Quebec: A Chronicle

Quebec: A Chronicle 1968-1972

A Last Post Special

Edited by Nick Auf der Maur and Robert Chodos

With a Postscript by Yvon Charbonneau, Louis Laberge and Marcel Pepin

James Lewis & Samuel, Publishers
Toronto
1972

ISBN 0-88862-024-1 (cloth)
        0-88862-025-x (paper)

Library of Congress Catalogue Card No. 72 90589

Design by Lynn Campbell

James Lewis & Samuel, Publishers
35 Britain Street
Toronto
Canada

Printed and bound in Canada

Contents

Foreword

There is room for a book which offers a reflective examination of recent developments in Quebec, a book which stands back from events and puts them in their larger context, relates them to the major trends in Quebec and world history, and tries to predict where they will lead.

There is room for such a book but this is not it, at least not except in a very peripheral way. This book is very much an interim report, a report that of necessity has no conclusion, and we hope that what it lacks in comprehensiveness and analytical depth it makes up for in immediacy. For each chapter is based on articles written for the *Last Post* magazine at the time of the events the chapter describes. In combining the articles into a book, we had to make some changes; awkward time references were rephrased, and errors that had crept through our editing staff were eliminated. We had overestimated the importance of some events and these sections were cut down or taken out, while others describing events whose importance we had underestimated were beefed up. An attempt was made too to smooth out jarring changes in tone caused by combining articles by two or more writers.

With all that, we found that the articles stood up remarkably well. Our coverage of the War Measures Act crisis, widely regarded at the time as the best article of its kind in French or English, has since been surpassed in thoroughness by numerous books on the subject, but it still reads as a good summary of what the government was trying to do. In the case of one article, Simone Chartrand's biography of her husband Michel, we found that the article stood up so well and its personal tone and character were so important to its effectiveness that it was impossible to tamper with it; it is included here in its original form. It has been gratifying to us that James Lewis and Samuel shared our view of the continuing validity of these and other articles and considered it worthwhile to publish them as a book.

The *Last Post* has developed simultaneously with the Quebec situation, and our best issues have often coincided with landmark events in Quebec. Our very first issue featured an article ("Quebec: Into the Streets," which forms the basis of Chapter 1) written in Montreal during the turbulent autumn of 1969, an article that had to be constantly updated almost until press time to take account of new developments. That set a pattern that has been repeated several times since—during the War Measures Act crisis of 1970, the *La Presse* conflict of 1971, and the Common Front strike of 1972.

Although the articles that make up this book are the work of at least a half-dozen different writers, there is one whose contribution deserves special mention. There is no English-language journalist in Montreal who has as many contacts at all levels from the government to the FLQ, is as knowledgeable about events in Quebec or can write as cogently about them as Nick Auf der Maur, and the *Last Post* has been very fortunate to have him as its Quebec editor. In saying that the perceptions, the colour and the overall tone of this book are essentially his, I am not trying to evade responsibility for its contents but simply giving credit where it is due.

Robert Chodos

I

The Failure of the Quiet Revolution

If the early sixties were the years of the Quiet Revolution in Quebec, the late sixties and early seventies were turning out to be the years of the Quiet Restoration.*

None of the governments that succeeded the Liberal administration of Jean Lesage after 1966 recaptured that administration's élan and utopian zeal. The occasional reformer who did come along, like Claude Castonguay, minister of social affairs under Robert Bourassa, was all the more conspicuous because he was so rare.

Patronage and corruption, which had never disappeared altogether, were back in full flower. Governments reverted to their pre-1960 role of welcomers of foreign capital and keepers in place of the native population. Party affiliations, which for a brief time had actually reflected political differences, didn't seem to mean much any more: thus one politician, Claude Wagner, could be mentioned as a possible leader of three different parties in the course of a single year. Unlike the defeat of the Union Nationale by the Lesage Liberals in 1960, the defeat of a latter-day Union Nationale government by the Bourassa Liberals in 1970 seemed merely the exchange of one gang for another. It was the traditional pattern: the government changed, virtually everything else remained the same.

Still, there were elements in the political situation that were distinctly not traditional. For while the regime appeared stagnant and archaic, the opposition was growing, vibrant and constantly in flux. At first it took the form of small political groups, student demonstrations, bombings, nationalist agitation; but by the 1970s it had reached into every level of society in Quebec, every aspect of politics, every facet of popular culture.

Le Journal de Montréal, a tabloid newspaper with non-

*This chapter is based on "Quebec: Into the Streets," by *Last Post* staff, *Last Post*, December 1969; and "The Road to Mont Laurier," by Nick Auf der Maur, *Last Post*, May 1972.

descript political loyalties, made a hero of Paul Rose of the Front de Libération du Québec. French-speaking hockey star Henri Richard criticized English-speaking coach Al MacNeil and all of a sudden hockey became a major political issue for Quebec sports columnists and fans. A new style of pop music expressed a strongly-felt collective identity.

After 1970, the chief parliamentary opposition party, in terms of popular vote and influence, was one advocating the political independence of Quebec. The separatists, a tiny minority only ten years earlier, had become a powerful force, attracting members from the most respectable classes of society—doctors, lawyers, economists, civil servants.

This parliamentary opposition was overshadowed by an even stronger, more radical, extraparliamentary one, based in the trade-union movement. When the unions moved into the forefront in 1971, they represented more than the renaissance of the French Canadian people; they also represented a serious movement for a new kind of society. They challenged not only the English domination of Quebec, but the political system as a whole.

These developments occurred rapidly, and no one could predict with certainty where they would lead next. But they had their roots in economic changes that had been taking place over two generations.

As recently as 1920, Quebec was still largely rural and backward. There had been some development in the textile and lumber-paper industries, by means first of British and then of American capital, but not enough to change the base of the value system or of social organization, as it had stood in essence since the battle on the Plains of Abraham.

Quebec is rich in natural resources—principally minerals, timber and water for hydroelectric power. In the eyes of investors, it had another crucial plus—an untapped supply of cheap labour. American capital began to move in and overtake the British and Anglo-Canadian interests. Starting in the thirties and accelerating through World War II and the postwar period, Quebec underwent its major industrial revolution.

Typical of the American entry into Quebec was Hollinger-Hanna, a consortium of U.S. steel companies that began exploiting the deposits of iron ore along Quebec's north shore in the late forties and early fifties. Hollinger-Hanna later consolidated its Canadian operations into the Iron Ore Company of Canada, which has since sent over 150,000,000 tons of ore to the Cleveland, Ohio, smelters of the Republic, National, Armco, Youngstown and Wheeling steel companies.

In order to attract the steel companies, the Union Nationale government of Maurice Duplessis negotiated a paltry one-cent-a-ton tariff on ore carried out of Quebec. A few years later, when Joey Smallwood negotiated 30 cents a ton from the same companies for iron ore exploitation in Newfoundland, he faced a chorus of critics accusing him of "selling out to American interests for virtually nothing."

From the same roots that provided Duplessis his soft words toward American investors sprang his use of the big stick against incipient trade unionism. In 1949, he viciously crushed the strike against the U.S.-owned Johns-Manville Co. at Asbestos, sending in waves of Quebec Provincial Police (virtually a private Union Nationale army at the time) to break up picket lines and run through truckloads of scabs. Asbestos set a pattern that was to be repeated throughout the 1950s.

As a result, American capital came into Quebec on its own terms, and the wages of the French worker stayed well below that of his English counterpart. This was reflected in the educational system, or rather systems. English schools were better equipped, more scientifically oriented, and better financed. French schools were characterized by poor teaching and clerical control at the lower levels, and by a stress on classical disciplines like Greek and Latin at the higher levels. Common professions for the better-off French were law, medicine and the Church.

Those who sought decent-paying jobs learned English, and educated their children to speak English. This applied even to the French upper-middle class, because to be a corporation lawyer, for example, one had to speak English.

The Union Nationale government, despite the aggressive, quasi-nationalist stance in favour of provincial autonomy that it frequently took against Ottawa, was a convenient ally for the English commercial and industrial elite. Since the government accepted the need to accommodate foreign capital and keep the mass of the population in a cheap labour pool, the St. James Street boys were more than happy to fill the Union Nationale coffers at election time—another key part of the strange alliance behind Duplessis.

Thus, the English commercial and industrial bosses and the branch managers of American capital maintained their domination over the French population by supporting a native class of *rois nègres* (former *Le Devoir* editor André Laurendeau's phrase in comparing the Quebec bourgeoisie to the black African chiefs who served colonialism).

The Union Nationale was re-elected time and again as a result of the backing of the rural areas (Montreal was preponderantly Liberal). In return, it supplied the rural areas with material assistance such as farm loans, road development, telephones, and various forms of patronage. On the cultural level, it protected the farmers and the Church from the centralizing Liberal influence of Ottawa.

By the late fifties, however, the shaky alliance supporting Duplessis was breaking down.

In 1957, a new alliance that was to dislodge the Union Nationale showed its muscle in a bitter, lost strike in the tiny Gaspesian mining town of Murdochville. Noranda Mines Ltd., a Canadian-owned, Toronto-based mining giant that controls a whole string of company towns across northern Quebec, began after World War II to develop the rich copper deposits of the Gaspesian interior. With the help of the provincial government, power lines were put up, roads were built, and the town of Murdochville (named after Noranda president J. Y. Murdoch) was created to service the company's mine and smelter.

From the beginning, the United Steelworkers of America had tried to organize in Murdochville, and Noranda had tried to keep them out. It had sanctioned a rival union, denied promotions and bonuses to Steelworkers leaders, and unilaterally announced a wage increase to undercut the organizing attempts. On March 8, 1957, the company fired Théo Gagné, the president of the Steelworkers local. Two days later, the workers went on strike.

The strike lasted six months, and was marked by frequent demonstrations, two deaths, and the very noticeable presence, by now common in Quebec strikes, of Premier Duplessis's police. The strikers attracted support from both branches of the divided Quebec labour movement, the

Quebec Federation of Labour (with which the United Steelworkers are affiliated) and the rival Canadian Catholic Confederation of Labour, as well as from liberal intellectuals like Pierre Elliott Trudeau of the *Cité Libre* group and journalists like Pierre Laporte of *Le Devoir*. Murdochville polarized Quebec society much as the Asbestos strike had eight years earlier.

The company succeeded in reopening the plant with a staff of strikebreakers and finally forced the strikers to capitulate. (Not until 1965 would the Steelworkers be certified in Murdochville.) But the alliance the strike had helped forge was on the ascendancy, and the apparently invincible Duplessis machine was crumbling. For the needs of capital were changing. Capital now demanded skilled labour and a government that provided technocrats to plan hydroelectric power projects and communications systems. It needed a new managerial elite.

The Quebec Liberal Party, meanwhile, was building the sort of team that would be able to reorient Quebec along these lines.

Maurice Duplessis, undisputed "Chef" of the Union Nationale for 23 years, died a quiet death in the Iron Ore Company of Canada's palatial guest house in Schefferville on September 18, 1959.

The Liberals, under former federal Northern Development and Natural Resources minister Jean Lesage, moved in with a promise to "open the window and air the place out." To the workers they promised reforms of the labour code and a revamped social welfare scheme. To the intellectuals and young technocrats they promised educational reform. To the investors and corporations, they promised a smooth administration and a host of skilled managers and technocrats.

On June 22, 1960, the Union Nationale was defeated. Lesage was in, and he delivered on the promises. The notaries and small-town politicians were replaced by a new generation of technocrats—young sociologists, economists, engineers and planners from the universities and the corporations. The change was called "The Quiet Revolution."

For two years Quebec experienced a period of rising confidence, as labour leaders, students, and technocrats defined the needs of their own particular sectors. Confidence peaked with the 1962 election. It was fought on the issue of whether or not to nationalize the hydroelectric power companies. Natural Resources Minister René Lévesque fought for nationalization and won. Lesage broke out the election slogan that raised eyebrows in Ottawa: *Maîtres Chez Nous*—Masters in Our Own House.

This meant that Quebec should produce its own engineers, set up its own laboratories, modernize its own schools, launch its own industries, and generally provide for the needs of its own people.

But while the government could give workers the right of collective bargaining, it could provide neither the wage hikes they demanded nor security against price increases. And while it could draw the blueprint for educational reforms, it could not pay for them.

The nationalization of Hydro may have seemed a proud moment, but it was perhaps not nationalization in the strict sense; for Quebec *bought* the companies from the private interests that controlled them. Surely Quebec could not buy back all of its sold and stolen resources. The Liberals had come in on a wave of rising expectations, but they could not ride its crest forever.

An example of how the economic domination of the American and Anglo-Canadian capitalists had perverted the social structure and served the English (17 per cent of the population) at the expense of the French (83 per cent) emerged in a study made by the Royal Commission on Bilingualism and Biculturalism. The study (which was leaked to the Montreal daily *La Presse* in 1968, two years before it was officially released) revealed that in Quebec, a Canadian of British origin, *unilingual,* earns an average yearly salary of $5,502. But a *bilingual* British Canadian earns an average of $4,772. A *bilingual* French Canadian earns $4,350, while a *unilingual* French Canadian earns $3,099.

This means that a *unilingual* British Canadian in Quebec earns $1,152 more a year than a *bilingual* French Canadian.

Furthermore, a British Canadian who is *unilingual* earns $730 more than a fully *bilingual* British Canadian in Quebec.

The report left unstated what this means in terms of bilingualism as a solution to the "national problem," but it did state this obvious conclusion: "In Quebec, it pays *not* to speak French."

The study further revealed that:

Quebec is the *only province in the country* in which a unilingual British Canadian earns more than a bilingual one.

Canadians of British origin have incomes 10 per-cent higher than the average in every province except Quebec, where they earn 40 per cent more than the average.

English managerial personnel in Quebec earn $6,234 more than English workers, whereas French Canadian managers earn $3,308 more than French Canadian workers.

The study also shows that a French Canadian who goes to university will up his income less than an English, Jewish or Italian Canadian who goes to university (almost invariably an English one)—demonstrating the economic advantages of English education for immigrants.

Finally, of fourteen national groups whose incomes were studied, the British earned the most, while the three lowest groups, from bottom up, were native Indians, Italians and French Canadians.

Not only are the Québécois, 83 per cent of the population, not Masters in their Own House, they are servants. And poorly paid ones at that.

The Liberals had ultimately failed to deliver, and the Union Nationale, revamped by its leader, Daniel Johnson, began capitalizing on the frustrated expectations and on the Liberals' neglect of the rural areas. In June 1966, the Liberals lost by a narrow margin to the Union Nationale, and the policy of low wages to attract foreign capital returned. But there were some disturbing statistics in the election returns: the Rassemblement pour l'Indépendance Nationale got 9 per cent of the vote.

In 1962, a few hundred students had demonstrated peacefully in front of the Canadian National Railways' head office in downtown Montreal. It was the first big nationalist demonstration of the sixties, and it was protesting the CNR's policy of not hiring French-speaking senior executives. The students burned a Canadian red ensign flag and an effigy of CNR president Donald Gordon.

The great "separatism" debate was on. Toronto theatre groups began inviting Quebec companies to cross the border and show off their cultural wares to the cognoscenti, and Berlitz started raking in a fortune.

The next year, the first Front de Libération Québécois (FLQ) blew up several of Her Majesty's royal mailboxes in English-speaking Westmount.

The FLQ got most of the headlines, but it was only one of a plethora of nationalist and left-wing groups that had started to spring up. In the early sixties nationalists of various hues grouped in the Alliance Laurentienne and later in the Rassemblement pour l'Indépendance Nationale (RIN). A socialist independence group, the Action Socialiste pour l'Indépendance du Québec (many of whose members had split with the Communist Party in the fifties over the national question), also was formed around that time.

The ASIQ and a succeeding group, the Mouvement Ouvrier pour la Libération Nationale, soon dissolved, with much of the membership going over to the RIN. But the latter party never progressed politically much beyond the centre. Its basic constituency was those who wanted to achieve the Liberals' unkept promise of *Maîtres Chez Nous* through different means. The first RIN members, according to surveys at the time, were the rising new middle class and academics, white-collar workers who wanted to reach decision-making levels in business.

Another new party was the Parti Socialiste du Québec (PSQ), the result of a schism over Quebec nationalism at the founding of the New Democratic Party in 1961. Neither the PSQ nor the NDP ever got off the ground in Quebec because of the split. However, various PSQ leaders such as Michel Chartrand and Jean-Marie Bedard were distinct influences in the left movement.

In 1964 Pierre Vallières, who had been a member of the *Cité Libre* group under Pierre Elliott Trudeau and Gérard Pelletier but had broken with them over their approach to the independence question, helped to form the Mouvement de Libération Populaire (MLP). The MLP, along with the earlier *Parti Pris* group, produced most of the new wave of left-wing thinkers in the province. Intellectually, the *Parti Pris* group was to have the most serious influence on the development of the left.

Factionalism crept into the MLP and it too disbanded. Some members went over to the PSQ, some—notably the group surrounding Mme Andrée Ferretti—joined the RIN, while Pierre Vallières and Charles Gagnon revived the FLQ.

A year later both wound up in jail, their home for the next four years or so.

It was a heady period for Quebec radicals. There were abundant issues, demonstrations and bombings. There were serious political groups, political groups that were filled with crazies, and political groups that were simply amusing. The Quebec student union, UGEQ, with strong anarchist tendencies, was at its peak.

The radical activists of the time were for the most part young students or dropouts, with an equal mixture of working- and middle-class backgrounds. Their political views and formation (or lack of them) varied from romantic Guevaraism to tough Algerian revolutionism; their most consistent common denominator was passionate nationalism.

The largest pro-independence party, the RIN, was sharply split into a distinct right and left. The left garnered most of the publicity and organized most of the actions, making the RIN a party that would take to the streets if necessary. Led by Mme Ferretti, the left held that since Quebec was controlled by foreign capital along with a domestic English elite, there could be no "independence" unless the whole socioeconomic system was reformed. "We're in a mortal struggle against all who contribute to our exploitation," Mme Ferretti repeated over and over again, "whether they be American imperialists, Canadian capitalists or the French Canadian bourgeoisie."

The growth of support for the independence movement also spawned another party. René Lévesque, who had built up a vast personal following during the Lesage administration, saw that cutting constitutional ties with Canada would enable the planning of a rational economy in Quebec and would open up more high positions for the native population. In the fall of 1967 he was forced out of the Liberal Party and formed the Mouvement Souveraineté-Association, aimed at a separate Quebec in a common-market association with Canada.

Lévesque's MSA grew, as disaffected Liberals and left-liberal nationalists rallied behind its charismatic leader. But it was only an interim organization, the first step toward a single, broad-based independence party. In 1968, the right-wing Ralliement National (led by Gilles Grégoire, a former federal Social Credit MP) united with the MSA to form the Parti Québécois.

In the meantime, the left-wingers had tried to take over the RIN. Pierre Bourgault fought them off and then took most of the RIN into the newly-formed PQ.

The far left formed something called the Comité Indépendance-Socialisme (CIS) as well as the Front de Libération Populaire (FLP), the latter meant vaguely to be the aboveground version of the FLQ.

The task of both the PQ and the extraparliamentary left was made easier by a crumbling and inept government in Quebec City.

The Union Nationale government, elected in 1966, was having difficulty combining its nationalistic *Québec d'Abord* (Quebec First) slogan with the attraction of more outside investment. Under the leadership of Daniel Johnson, author of *Equality or Independence*, it had maintained a tough nationalist image, highlighted in 1967 by the visit of President de Gaulle, particularly by his "Québec Libre" speech in Montreal.

Premier Johnson, or "Danny Boy" as he was fondly called, managed remarkably well on the surface. While attempting to be all things to all men, he bounced around from crisis to crisis with his Cheshire cat smile. He always looked as if he had just swallowed the canary—and he generally had. But Johnson, who could draw some fire away from the independence groups, died in office in September 1968. The less skilled, more "moderate" Jean-Jacques Bertrand took over, and his nineteen-month premiership was to be one of the most chaotic periods in the recent history of Quebec.

Two weeks after Johnson's death, the lid blew off in the CEGEPs, Quebec's network of government-run community colleges. Creation of the CEGEPs had been one of the most important educational reforms of the sixties. It had been one of the chief recommendations of the Parent Report, a weighty, historic document commissioned by the Lesage government almost immediately upon taking office.

The CEGEPs were intended to replace the old *collèges classiques,* whose curriculum had consisted of Latin, Greek and Thomist philosophy. These new institutions were to be very different. They were to turn out the technicians so badly needed in the new, confident Quebec, and to serve as pre-university way stations for the apprentices of the new elite.

In 1967 the Union Nationale government finally got the first CEGEPs off the ground, but they were a rush job. They were set up in physically inadequate, converted *collèges classiques*, administrative organization was virtually nonexistent, and their creation had not been co-ordinated with other aspects of government planning. Far more students than expected chose the pre-university course, although university places for them did not exist. Worst of all, the jobs the CEGEPs had been created to fill did not exist either.

Two years later, Industry and Commerce Minister Jean-Paul Beaudry admitted, "These schools were set up to raise the technological competence of our labour force. But these activities were not co-ordinated with those of the department of Industry and Commerce . . . now students are clamouring and we are just catching up in being able to provide jobs for them."

In September 1968, sixteen new CEGEPs were added to the seven opened a year earlier. But on October 8, 1968, CEGEP Lionel-Groulx in the Montreal suburb of Ste-Thérèse was occupied; within a few days the revolt had spread throughout the system, as students struck, occupied their buildings, and forced the schools to close. Two weeks later, 10,000 *CEGEPiens* were in the streets demanding a less repressive education, a new French-language university, and jobs.

But soon they were back in classes, with conditions, if anything, worse than before. The government's response was to intensify repression (student leaders were expelled, newspapers closed, public assemblies banned) and to step up its search for investment. ("I intend to make trips to the U.S.—often," Beaudry said. "Possibly Germany will be on the itinerary in the next few months. I'll go anywhere if there is a chance of gaining something for Quebec.")

The CEGEP students provided most of the troops for the series of large demonstrations which, along with a renewed series of FLQ bombings, marked the next year. The specific targets of these demonstrations varied, but the participants, the mood, and the underlying purpose were the same. Some of the larger demonstrations were:

Opération McGill. McGill University, the prestigious

English-language institution in downtown Montreal, has long been regarded as a symbol of English privilege in Quebec. In early 1969, the Ligue pour l'Intégration Scolaire (LIS), a group demanding French unilingualism in education, the FLP, the CIS, the Montreal Central Council of the Confederation of National Trade Unions, CEGEP students, and a handful of turncoat McGill students led by political science professor Stanley Gray organized a campaign demanding that McGill be turned into a French-language university. The campaign was to culminate in a demonstration March 28. The McGill administration, the provincial government (with the significant support of PQ leader René Lévesque) and the police led the counter-campaign, with the help of hysterical radio reports and newspaper stories. People were arrested on the street and in taverns. On the eve of the march, the army was placed on alert. The demonstration took place, ten thousand people marched to the gates of McGill, the violence was minor, and the hysteria died down.

Opération Congrès. This demonstration, in June 1969, brought the usual activists together with dissatisfied teachers and civil servants outside the Coliseum in Quebec City, where a Union Nationale congress was confirming Jean-Jacques Bertrand in the party leadership. It was eventually broken up with tear gas and a series of arrests.

St-Léonard. In 1968, the Mouvement pour l'Intégration Scolaire (later the Ligue pour l'Intégration Scolaire) was formed to contest school board elections in the east-end, mixed-French-and-Italian Montreal suburb of St-Léonard, on a platform of making French the only language of education. With the vast majority of immigrants to Quebec integrating into the English community, the MIS argued, the French were in danger of becoming a minority in their own province. The MIS candidates won, and their attempts to implement their platform led to a series of pamphlets, editorials, meetings, demonstrations and riots over the next two years. At one demonstration, in September 1969, tear gas was used, fights broke out between French and Italian youths, the riot act was read, and three people, including LIS leader Raymond Lemieux, were charged with sedition.

Murray Hill. The new wave that hit Quebec politics in 1960 was not restricted to the Lesage Liberals; that same year Jean Drapeau was elected mayor of Montreal on promises to "clean up the city" of its corruption, provide better services for its citizens and generally bring progress to the metropolis. Drapeau succeeded in making Montreal a showcase with its stainless-steel skyline, shiny new subway and midriver Expo, but not in providing such frills as low-cost housing. Among the groups that had become disenchanted with Drapeau by 1969 were Montreal's taxi drivers and its police. On October 7, 1969, the police struck for wage parity with Toronto. In the late afternoon the taxi drivers demonstrated in front of City Hall in support of the cops, then marched to the Murray Hill Limousine Service garage. Among their chief grievances were the monopolies granted to Murray Hill. Buses were burned; a sniper started firing at the demonstrators from the roof of the garage; one of the demonstrators started firing back from another roof; several demonstrators were wounded; and an undercover Quebec Provincial policeman, Cpl. Robert Dumas, was killed. Then the demonstrators moved on to Murray Hill hotel pickup points, to Drapeau's luxury restaurant, *Le Vaisseau d'Or*, to McGill University, to IBM, and through the main shopping district, smashing windows and looting stores. With another demonstration threatened three days later, the army was brought in to keep order.

Bill 63. The government's language-of-education bill, Bill 63, was intended as a final solution to the St-Léonard problem. It said that English-language education would be provided wherever there was demand for it. The English were solidly behind the bill, but large parts of the French community were opposed, and they formed the Front du Québec Français, uniting more than a hundred groups ranging from the FLP and the Montreal Central Council of the CNTU through the LIS to the conservative nationalist St-Jean-Baptiste Society. The Bill 63 demonstrations, while peaceful, were the largest in Quebec in recent years; thirty thousand people marched in Montreal on October 29, 1969, and the same number demonstrated outside the National Assembly in Quebec City two nights later. Nevertheless, Bill 63 was passed.

Vallières-Gagnon. This was an anti-repression march on November 7, 1969, organized mostly by the FLP. It demanded the release of Pierre Vallières and Charles Gagnon, who at that point had been in jail for three years, and the resignation of Rémi Paul, the new Quebec justice minister responsible for "anti-terrorist" measures and sedition charges, along with the usual range of demands like a French-language McGill, a unilingual St-Léonard and the repeal of Bill 63. The demonstrators marched to Montreal City Hall and then to the St. James Street financial district, where they threw rocks and smashed windows. Vallières and Gagnon were eventually released by the new Liberal government in 1970.

Vallières-Gagnon was the last of the big demonstrations. Drapeau pushed through an anti-demonstration bylaw that succeeded in imposing an uneasy quiet on the city. Two hundred women defied the bylaw in late November and were arrested, but the explosive mood of the early fall did not recur.

The CIS had long since fallen apart; the LIS and the FLP were soon to follow. Flamboyant leaders like Raymond Lemieux and Stanley Gray dropped out of sight. The left seemed in disarray. But under the surface, it was also gaining a certain maturity. Marginal fringe-group politics were increasingly being replaced by the activities of citizens' committees and trade-union politicization. In early 1970, the Montreal citizens' committees formed an alliance, the Front d'Action Politique (FRAP), to fight Mayor Drapeau in the October civic elections. Larger and larger portions of the population started to become involved—bus drivers, miners, construction workers, teachers and nurses.

The aspect of the 1969 demonstrations that had the most lasting significance was the participation of the Montreal Central Council of the Confederation of National Trade Unions, led by Michel Chartrand. For it presaged the growing militancy and political consciousness of the trade-union movement in Quebec and its later position as the centre of the political opposition to the regime.

With the advent of the Lesage Liberals and the Quiet Revolution in 1960, the union movement, especially the CNTU (the successor to the old Canadian Catholic Confederation of Labour), underwent a period of major growth. In less than a decade, the CNTU doubled its membership, mostly in the public and para-public sectors such as the civil service and the hospitals. During that time, the CNTU, originally founded as a Catholic alternative to "dangerous social tendencies" of American-supported unions, maintained its intense rivalry towards the Quebec Federation of Labour. The QFL in turn always suspected the Liberals of favouritism towards the CNTU.

Another conflict developed within the CNTU itself. Marcel Pepin, who had succeeded Jean Marchand as president of the CNTU in 1965, had little use for the sort of political action that Chartrand engaged in, and kept trying to dislodge Chartrand from his powerful position as president of the Montreal Central Council. But even the Pepin wing of the CNTU acknowledged the need for union activity outside the established framework of collective bargaining. The union's 1969 manifesto, *The Second Front*, called on union members to establish co-operatives and organize on the consumer front. More hesitantly, it called for political action as well.

By 1970, amid all the national and social ferment in the province, a common interest was developing within the ranks of the CNTU, the QFL and the Quebec Teachers Corporation, brought on by common experiences. Instead of engaging in fratricidal combat, the unions got used to co-operating. They helped to found *Québec-Presse*, the fighting weekly tabloid; started co-ops; and declared common fronts on various issues.

There was one other serious new force building up. By the time a provincial election was called for April 29, 1970, René Lévesque's Parti Québécois had a membership of 41,000; it would grow to 85,000 by election day. A poll taken for the Montreal daily *La Presse* three weeks before the election showed the PQ with the support of almost a quarter of the population—and less than one percentage point behind the front-running Liberals. Many of the rest were undecided. The last attempts to dismiss the PQ as a fringe group were laid to rest.

Instead, the English business community let surface its darkest nightmares about hooded separatists riding to power in Quebec City. The Montreal *Star*, in an editorial by editor Gerald Clark, said that Lévesque, while himself an honourable man, would be the "Kerensky of the Quebec revolution" and would give way to the inevitable Lenins, Trotskys and Stalins waiting in the wings. The Royal Trust Company packed some securities into a Brinks truck and pointed it in the direction of Toronto—making sure a Montreal *Gazette* photographer was there to get pictures. The federal Liberal Party contributed a pamphlet, *Quoi de Neuf?* (What's New?), "proving" that Quebec got more out of Confederation than it put in. (The PQ countered with a pamphlet of its own "proving" the opposite, pointing out that the Liberal effort had taken into account the salaries paid by the government-owned Canadian National Railways to Quebecers, but not the fares paid by Quebecers to the CNR.)

The scare campaign worked. The PQ kept its twenty-four per cent of the vote, but most of the undecideds went Liberal. In what became known in radical and separatist mythology as "le coup d'état électoral," the Liberals won 72 of the 108 National Assembly seats, although their share of the popular vote was reduced to 45 per cent from the 47 per cent they had got in the 1966 elections, which they lost. The PQ, with a quarter of the vote, only managed seven seats, mostly in the working-class districts of Montreal's East End. The Union Nationale was reduced to a rump, while Social Credit, already a power federally in Quebec, cashed in on rural poverty and discontent and won 12 seats on 12 per cent of the vote. The discrepancy between the PQ's popularity in the province and its tiny representation in the Assembly was to grow into a major issue, convincing people of the inequity of the electoral system.

The new premier of Quebec was 36-year-old Robert Bourassa, who had been chosen for the succession to Lesage by the federal Liberal Party and the powerful and wealthy Simard family, into which he had married. Bourassa's campaign was based on a promise of 100,000 jobs and a slogan of "le fédéralisme rentable"—profitable federalism. If the slogan implied no deep ideological commitment to the federal state, that was not surprising, for when the Parti Québécois had been formed eighteen months earlier, Bourassa had toyed with the idea of joining it. The original PQ economic platform had been written in his basement, on his typewriter, with his help.

II

Cabbies and Mail-Truck Drivers: 'Vous allez fighter'

The scene inside the Salon Funéraires Alfred Dallaires wasn't exactly sombre.* To be sure, the relatives—workers in their Sunday suits come to bury the dead taxi driver—lent an air of traditional respectability. But there was a singular tone that morning of March 18, 1969, at the funeral parlor in east-end Montreal.

A voice on a tape recorder said, "I read a lot now; three newspapers a day, lots of little booklets, because the more one develops on the level of personal thinking . . . the more one is able to live life fully, to protect himself against things and all that they, society, try to inculcate in you . . . like all the superfluous 'needs' pushed by advertising. People today are very perturbed by the useless things pushed by the ads . . . a lot of people don't have the preparation . . . to resist those things they can't afford . . . ."

The voice was that of the man in the coffin. The crucifix on top of the coffin was covered over with a flag and a picture of Che Guevara.

The coffin was carried out by four men employed by the funeral parlor and two men employed by the Montreal Police Department. The funeral director was told the police were needed for "security reasons."

The cortege departed, followed by 150 taxis stretching into a mile-long line, packed with relatives, working men, and an incredible array of radicals—passionate rebels, old-fashioned revolutionaries, run-of-the-mill socialists, misty-eyed Trotskyists, pulpit-pounding Maoists.

It stopped at the monument to the Patriote Chenier, a leader of the 1837 rebellion against British colonialism. Speeches by Mario Brière and Gaston Therrien, veteran cab-

---

*This chapter is based on "Lessons on Fighting City Hall: A Study of Montreal's 'Mouvement de Libération du Taxi,'" by Nick Auf der Maur, *Last Post*, June 1970; and "The Lapalme Boys: 'On Veut nos Jobs'" by Nick Auf der Maur, *Last Post*, September 1971.

bies, blared from loudspeakers mounted atop one car.

The cortege started again, picking up speed, until it was moving at 60 miles an hour; long-haired and crop-haired people hung out the windows, waving red flags and clenched fists. The cortege was going too fast—but the hearse was being driven by one of the policemen, who wanted the man buried quickly, without incident.

The red flags were out again at the Cimetière de l'Est. Two men played Swiss alphorns. Gaston Miron, one of Quebec's best-known poets, recited. The coffin was lowered and the large crowd sang the *Internationale*.

"I want to die in the simplest way possible," the voice on the tape recorder on top of the coffin said, "that is to say I don't want the traditional farce of religious rites as they exist in Quebec. And when they bury me, to paraphrase Brel, I want people to laugh, to sing, to amuse themselves like crazy when they put me in the hole."

The funeral of Germain Archambault was different from other funerals, but it was part of something that was happening in Quebec. For Germain Archambault was the leader of one of the most unlikely, romantic, earthy, and militant labour organizations in North America—the Mouvement de Libération du Taxi. While most of Quebec's more traditional labour groups stayed aloof, the MLT participated actively in the big demonstrations of the late sixties; a curious alliance grew up between the taxi drivers and the student militants. Along with the struggle of the unemployed mail-truck drivers who became known as "les gars de Lapalme," the rise of the MLT was an early indication of the new mood that was later to sweep through large sections of the Quebec working class.

Taxi drivers have often, with some justification, been considered unorganizable. Up until 1964, taxi drivers in Montreal tried—and failed—no fewer than 57 times to form some sort of union or association. There was a brotherhood set up in the thirties; something called the Union Internationale des Chauffeurs de Taxi in 1940; an effort by the Teamsters in the fifties; attempts by the old Canadian Catholic Confederation of Labour—all of them short-lived, crushed quickly by the owners or ground down slowly by the supposed impossibility of organizing taxi drivers.

The lot of the Montreal taxi driver today is not much better than it was in the forties, or even the twenties. The average driver has to put in 70 to 80 hours a week, in the worst traffic conditions in Canada, and is lucky if he manages to make a hundred dollars in the good seasons. He has no sick leave, vacation, pension rights or even unemployment insurance.

To begin with, there are too many taxis in the city, too many drivers, too many unemployed people, too many crooks.

Around the end of the war, well-off Montrealers were heard to complain that there were not enough taxis around. People sometimes had to walk blocks or wait in the rain for a cab. At that time, there were a total of 765 taxis in the city proper, or one per 1,388 inhabitants. The civic administration, headed by the fat and flamboyant Mayor Camillien Houde, acted swiftly to alleviate the problem. Houde, fresh from a stunning election victory following his release from a Second World War internment camp (for opposing conscription), put his city executive council chairman, J.O. Asselin, in charge of an inquiry. In March 1946, Asselin announced that there were not enough cabs in the city. He pointed out that New York had one hack per 665 population, Toronto one per 953. He opened up the previously frozen number of permits, bringing a brief end to permit speculation.

City taxi users were pleased, although there were some unkind cuts alleging that the Diamond Taxi Company had been allowed to grow to almost monopolistic proportions. In 1970 there were 5,402 licensed taxis on Montreal Island, or one for every 350 inhabitants (Toronto and New York ratios remained constant). And, an interesting historical footnote: at the 1969 House of Commons Transport Committee hearings, the Diamond Taxi Company was represented by E.T. Asselin, son of J.O. and a former Liberal MP whose alleged involvement in school land deals led to a rapid termination of his political career.

As mentioned earlier, there had been numerous attempts to organize drivers into a united force to improve their conditions. These efforts were always doomed to failure because nobody really understood the industry—the service or the servants or their problems. But in 1964 a book published by the left-wing magazine and publishing outfit *Parti Pris* appeared, entitled *Le Taxi: Métier de Crève-Faim* (The taxi business, a trade of the starving). The author was Germain

Archambault, an intense man in his mid-forties, who became Montreal's chief taxi militant and strategist.

He was a veteran driver who got forced into the business when his small grocery-store-cum-hot-dog-stand went bankrupt in Joliette. Before that he had dabbled in trade unionism and, in his youth, had been an activist in the wartime Bloc Populaire, as had Pierre Elliott Trudeau, Michel Chartrand, Jean Drapeau and any other French Canadian who had a head on his shoulders.

But by 1964 he had settled into his adopted trade and come to enjoy it. He was tough and ruddy looking, complete with the rough edges that marked him as a member of the working class. He was proud of his métier and of the fact that he knew the city streets inside out and provided a good service. Still, the hours, the working conditions, the injustices and the monopolies rankled him.

A compulsively energetic man, barely five-foot four, he devoted most of his spare time to researching and writing about the taxi business. He hoped his book would expose it all as Upton Sinclair's *The Jungle* had exposed Chicago's meat-packing plants, and, confident in the Drapeau administration's sense of justice, he expected a much-needed and thorough over-haul of the system. After all, Archambault reasoned, Jean Drapeau had been involved in the Bloc Populaire, and in 1960 taxi drivers had helped the reform candidate ferry voters to the polls.

The book came out. Nobody paid much attention to it and nothing happened.

At first Archambault was dejected, but soon, even though his health was poor, he began organizing. Organization was the only thing that would help the taxi drivers. It was slow at first but by the spring of 1967, drivers showed up at the Casa d'Italia restaurant and formed the Comité d'Entre'aide Sociale des Chauffers de Taxi de Montréal.

Three days later, on April 13, 1967, Germain Archambault and three committee members went off to City Hall to see Lucien Saulnier and present their complaints. For a starter, they wanted an end to "Sputniks" (unlicensed cabs from outside working within city limits) and a uniform dome light to distinguish Montreal cabs. Saulnier, the city executive committee chairman, promised he would act.

Archambault went on organizing with great zeal. He

wanted to form a union, set up a social centre for drivers and elaborate a program. He wanted to diminish the transient aspect of the business by helping drivers gain a sense of dignity and pride in their work. He met Expo officials and got them to enlarge the taxi area at La Ronde. The committee started its own magazine, *Le Fiacre*.

Montreal taxi drivers were at last developing a united voice and articulating their grievances. It rapidly became evident that the drivers held at least one thing in common—their antagonism towards the Murray Hill Limousine Service Ltd.

Murray Hill held all sorts of privileges and monopolies; it had the lucrative airport concession, deals with the major hotels, prime downtown public parking spaces for its tourist buses, access to the City's Mount Royal Park, tolerance from the police when double-parked in front of busy hotels, and a fat charter business. In addition, Murray Hill picked up passengers on call from private homes and ran what amounted to a taxi service with several hundred vehicles even though it didn't own a single municipal permit.

Germain Archambault flailed away at Murray Hill. The committee issued tracts and pamphlets. And grew. But after that first meeting with Lucien Saulnier, the city refused any further encounters.

In the early fall of 1967, the Comité called a meeting to consider the situation. About 200 drivers crammed into the slightly derelict Bar des Arts on Ste-Catherine Street East.

The next day, Montreal newspapers reported there was "dissatisfaction" among the city's cab-driving fraternity.

Ten days later, 1,200 dissatisfied taxi drivers assembled at an East End school hall during the rush hour to denounce Murray Hill and the civic administration. The speeches, including a reasoned if vociferous analysis from Archambault and intense diatribes from Greek and Italian spokesmen, resulted in a call for action.

"On veut justice!" came the cries. "A l'Hôtel de Ville! We want to talk with Drapeau!"

Twelve hundred enraged cabbies headed towards City Hall. "We want Drapeau, we want Saulnier!" they cried. The police guarded City Hall and nobody came out or went in. As word spread over car radios, more cabs arrived, surrounding the old Victorian building in a sea of unmatched dome lights.

"Don't honk!" someone shouted. That was the signal for the horns to begin playing incessantly, at first sounding the trumpeter's "charge" from the Montreal Forum, and then building up into a crescendo, a massive and collective foghorn. A warning signal. The first of the big Montreal taxi demonstrations had started.

"This is useless," Archambault said after a time, "there is nothing more to do here. Let's disperse."

Fifteen or sixteen hundred cabs moved off in all directions. And the urban taxi guerrilla was born.

Bands of taxis, with sometimes as many as 300 cars, careened around the city, disrupting downtown traffic, making the Murray Hill dispatchers at the hotels nervous.

Murray Hill limousines were harassed. Taxis followed the big green and white buses. Some tires were slashed. The taxi bands artfully avoided police patrols sent out to intercept them as individual cabs reported all police activity through the radio network. The noisy, sometimes frenzied demonstration was entirely spontaneous. It went on for hours and finally petered out about 4:30 in the morning.

The demonstration was judged to be a huge success. Archambault reasoned that while authorities may not have paid much attention to his book, at least they would have to pay attention now.

The Comité d'Entre'aide Sociale des Chauffeurs de Taxi de Montréal, flushed with success and boasting 1,500 members, opened a combination office-social centre on Fullum Street. Unfortunately, a few days later, in early October, Germain Archambault suffered a heart attack that laid him up for a considerable time and forced him into relative inactivity.

But there were others to take over—Noel Boutin, Denis Chrétin, Robert Monet and Guy Vincent.

Around the beginning of 1968, they switched their focus onto the activities of the fleet operations. In Montreal, about half of all taxis are owned by about a dozen individuals or companies who, along with smaller owners, rent the cars out to the taxi drivers at rates averaging $10 to $16 a twelve-hour shift. The Comité thought these rates excessive and organized a strike against Gold Circle Limited, a fleet operator with 40 to 50 cabs. The strike spread to Gamma Co. Ltd., Martin Station Service and others.

The taxi business being what it is, the strike was hard to enforce. Scabs were plentiful and taxis were hard to keep off the road, since they operated out of so many different garages and locations.

The strike proved ineffectual, although a few converts were made.

Gaston Therrien, later an MLT activist, recalled: "I was cruising along Sherbrooke and a car full of guys pulled up. 'Haven't you heard about the strike?' they asked. 'Hell, if there's a strike, I'm in it too.' It wasn't time to argue."

Because of the wrecked strike, the dashed hopes and the loss of Archambault's effervescent enthusiasm, the Comité d'Entre'aide floundered.

A riotous meeting at the Plateau Hall in Lafontaine Park forced the executive to resign. It was spring and there was great tumult, but alas, the committee died.

However, because of the depth of bitterness, the general taxi movement in the city proved to be resilient. Although little had been accomplished in the way of concrete gains, a few individuals with a great deal of optimism and grandiose plans came to the fore. And then began one of the more bizarre episodes in the history of the city's beleaguered taxi industry.

It was still spring when a former CNTU organizer turned taxi driver by the name of Louis Joseph decided the time had come to organize a genuine union. He, along with a small group, also decided that if it was going to be done, it had to be done properly.

They started off by announcing their intentions at a press conference at the Queen Elizabeth Hotel, complete with open bar for the journalists. That's the usual procedure at most press conferences, but then again most people who hold press conferences have a bit of power, not to mention money. They chalked up a $400 debt.

Since it was going to be a genuine union, they needed full-time organizers. That cost them $150 a week for the president, $125 for the vice-president.

A general convention was set up for July 14, Bastille Day.

At the beginning, the Syndicat des Chauffeurs de Taxi de Montréal was financed by personal savings and loans.

However, Louis Joseph had a stroke of genius. The budding union would organize a $5,000 lottery.

Since sales didn't go too well, it was decided to organize the Queen of the Taxis contest. Fifteen girls were recruited from a modelling agency. The idea was that they would sell lottery tickets, for a commission, and the one who sold the most tickets would become Queen of the Taxis. A grand prize featuring a trip to Europe was mentioned.

A Queen of the Taxis lottery float replete with coloured lights and frills was constructed. It was greeted with amused looks from taxi drivers and passersby as it was towed through the downtown area and to the garages and stands, but nevertheless, ticket sales picked up a bit.

An accountant was hired ($125) and the union went to the University of Montreal for a marketing research man. They got an industrial relations graduate instead. Fresh out of school, he ended up pushing lottery tickets to students and UGEQ.

Meanwhile, the union organizers were trying to interest the Confederation of National Trade Unions, the Quebec Federation of Labour and the Canadian Labour Congress to help out. Louis Joseph, accompanied by one of the lottery princesses, even went down to New York to see the AFL-CIO.

By the time the big Bastille Day convention rolled around, the union was deep in debt (the lawyer alone was owed $3,000). However, in their search for prestige, the organizers lined up Robert Bourassa of the Liberal Party, Gérard Rancourt of the QFL and Mathias Rioux of the militant Montreal teachers' association to speak. The convention was held at the Queen Elizabeth Hotel.

About forty curious drivers turned up to see what was happening. Aside from the speeches, there was very little happening, and the drivers weren't impressed. The delegates voted to fire the president, but he refused to resign. By the time the Queen of the Taxis was supposed to be named everybody had lost interest. The SCTM died a natural death.

The taxi drivers were left without a movement. But the sense of frustration, of impotence, of outrage persisted.

In the late summer of 1968, a small group of disgruntled drivers, still smarting from past experiences but more militant than ever, gathered together at regular meetings to discuss "what must be done." They came into contact with other radical activists, mostly students and the "social animators" that abound in Montreal. Regular meetings were held, usually at the end of night shifts, around 3 a.m., in a little shack located in the school yard of l'Ecole des Beaux Arts.

At the beginning of September, the new group invited Germain Archambault to come out of his semi-retirement and help with the organization. Archambault proposed that the group be called the Mouvement de Libération du Taxi.

The fall of 1968 proved to be a time of general unrest in Quebec. The St-Léonard affair was in gestation, striking Domtar workers occupied a factory, and the CEGEP students launched their "October Revolution." Militancy was in the air.

There seemed to be an endless series of demonstrations, big and small. Newspapers were full of stories about "contestation" and the growth of the independence movement. Strikes, legal and wildcat, appeared to be more frequent. And the bombs of the FLQ were starting to be heard again.

MLT spokesmen toured the city, visiting occupied schools, picket lines and separatist party conventions. The first public manifestation of the MLT was a demonstration of solidarity with striking Liquor Board employees, led by taxis flying red banners.

The MLT was installed in a St-Denis Street office where it started producing tracts, pamphlets and documents denouncing the Murray Hill monopoly. One of the survivors of the old SCTM proposed that they revive an old Comité d'Entre'aide plan to block off the airport in protest. "Le scandale Murray Hill" became a rallying point for left-wing activists. It was ideal, a microcosm of everything wrong in Quebec.

Murray Hill was owned by an English-speaking capitalist, Charles Hershorn, who lived in Westmount luxury. For $60,000 he held the exclusive airport concession, depriving honest working men of millions of dollars in revenue yearly, the drivers said. The contract was granted by the federal government. The $60,000 payment, according to the MLT, wasn't enough to cover the expenses required to police the airport to keep Montreal taxis out.

On top of it all, owner Hershorn treated (and still treats)

his employees scandalously. Drivers (who are mostly classified as hotel doormen for labour law purposes) earn $1.20 an hour with overtime only after 60 hours a week. Most of his drivers put in a minimum of 70 hours a week. Hershorn has successfully fought off repeated attempts to bring in a union. (One Murray Hill driver has two framed letters in his home, one from the Federal Labour Relations Board, the other from the provincial board. Each letter refers his complaint about getting less than the legal wage rate to the other board. "What the hell," he says, "it's the only job I can get now at my age.")

In addition, drivers have to pay the costs for any minor accidents they incur.

One argument particularly elicited sympathy from French Canadians, and that was that nothing could be done about Murray Hill because of conflicting jurisdictions. The federal government runs the airport, the Provincial Transportation Board licenses the firm's operations, municipal regulations were being flouted. This prompted one left-wing paper to write: "Murray Hill knows this [jurisdictional] jungle like the Viet Cong knows the Mekong Delta and, on this terrain, hasn't tasted defeat up until now."

The MLT also alleged that Hershorn contributes to the Liberal Party, a charge supported by Frank Howard, federal New Democratic MP for Skeena. At the same time they pointed out that Lucien Hétu, former director general of services for the City of Montreal, is now retired and sitting on the board of directors of Murray Hill. It's also said Murray Hill has excellent relations with the Quebec Transportation Board.

October 30 was the date selected for the airport blockade. The MLT solicited student support. The idea was to fill taxis with supporters and drive out to the airport to block access roads. Archambault said they would shut down the airport for two, three, five days if necessary. The Murray Hill monopoly must be broken.

On the day of the demonstration, a few hundred taxis showed up at the University of Montreal. Others picked up students at McGill and various CEGEPs. In all about 700 cabs converged on the airport from different parts of the city.

A large group of students and drivers, on foot and waving

red flags, confronted the police contingent guarding Canada's biggest airport. Molotov cocktails flew and within minutes the Murray Hill depot was littered with burning cars and buses. The skirmishing and blockade lasted for about three hours, witnessed by crowds of arriving passengers who couldn't get out. Murray Hill was forced to take its vehicles off the roads, and few passengers managed to get to the airport.

Buses and limousines on the roads were forced to a stop by taxi guerrillas. Passengers were politely asked to disembark and then the vehicle was set ablaze.

Once again bands of taxis roamed city streets.

"Dorval [the airport] was a liberating experience," admitted one veteran. The federal government announced it would review the Murray Hill contract.

The demonstration became a national story and the MLT achieved overnight prominence. Sympathizers organized a benefit for the movement at the Paul Sauvé arena. More than 3,000 people showed up for the TAXICHAUD and heard some of Quebec's top artists—Robert Charlebois, Tex, Pauline Julien, Raymond Lévesque, Le Jazz Libre du Québec and Yvon Deschamps.

In the following months, outside elements departed from the organization and the MLT settled down to looking after its constituency.

The MLT embarked on a research program to study the needs of taxi drivers, their family budgets and the general transportation system in the area. (In December 1969, during hearings by the House of Commons Transport Committee inquiry into ground transport at airports, observers judged the MLT brief as more solid, better researched, better presented and better written than the one prepared by the City of Montreal.)

In the meantime, Germain Archambault continued to proselytize in the cafes and bars where taxi drivers hang out.

"Germain knew he was about to die," said Gaston Therrien of the MLT, "but this rancour and frustration about the taxi business made him want to leave with a *grand coup*."

In March 1969 he was found dead inside his taxi cab parked at a stand in Phillips Square. Doctors had told him he should cut down on his 70-hour work week and other activities because of his weak heart.

Hundreds of his colleagues took the spring morning off to mourn his death. His widow and three children were surprised at the presence at the funeral of all manner of separatist radicals.

The MLT continued its education and recruiting efforts throughout the summer, meeting every Tuesday. On Tuesday, October 7, 1969, the members gathered at their Garnier Street office to mull over a letter received the previous day from City Executive Committee Chairman Lucien Saulnier. The letter was a response to the MLT's umpteenth request for a meeting to discuss their grievances. For the umpteenth time, Saulnier turned down the request and said, in the letter dated October 3: "Je crois, en effet, qu'actuellement, il y a trop de dialogue pour ce qu'il y a d'action." (Roughly translated: I think there's too much talk going on for there to be any action.)

By 1:30 in the afternoon, most of those present were talking about the strike by city policemen. City Hall and news management being what they are in Montreal, there was absolutely no forewarning that such a strike was even remotely possible, much less imminent. The radio said, yes, there was a strike, that thousands of cops were gathered at the city-owned Paul Sauvé arena, a favourite spot for strike meetings. It took several hours for most people to get over their incredulity.

Dozens of sympathizers drifted by during the course of the discussion in the MLT office, which ended up centring on what, if anything, the organization should do about it. A few of the members went over to the Paul Sauvé arena to see what was up. They reported that the police were royally pissed off at the Drapeau-Saulnier administration. There appeared to be common assent. It was decided a show of solidarity in front of City Hall was in order. A convoy went down to Old Montreal and honked horns in front of the Victorian building. Other taxis showed up.

The flotilla of cabs went off through the downtown area. "Down with Murray Hill!" became the cry.

It didn't take long for the drivers and their radical friends to gather outside the Murray Hill garage. And it didn't take long for the fires to start or the shotguns to fire.

Before it was over, at least 30 people, most of them taxi drivers, were wounded. An undercover Quebec Provincial policeman, milling with the demonstrators, was killed by a shotgun blast. (A coroner's inquest failed to place responsibility for the death, although it was shown that several Murray Hill employees were armed with shotguns. One demonstrator went home to fetch a .303 and returned the fire.)

One of the wounded was Marc Carbonneau, a veteran taxi driver. A Murray Hill sniper hit him in the rear with a blast of buckshot. Doctors removed about 50 pellets from his buttocks and thighs. The experience, he later confided to friends, helped convince him to join the FLQ the next year and kidnap James Cross, the British trade official.

The crowd left and made its way to the city's main commercial area. The predominantly English-owned commercial area—the stores that sell all those "useless things pushed by the ads"—were fair game for the crowd that gathered to watch.

Again the MLT shot into nation-wide prominence, as the villains, of course. In December 1969 there was another attempt to set up a union for the Montreal taxi industry. This one was the work of the Canadian Federation of Independent Associations, a formation of company unions that specializes in keeping real unions out.

The CFIA had made inroads into the transportation field before. Back in 1961, when drivers were able to boast a $58.38 paycheque for 70 hours' work, the Teamsters had tried to organize a union at Murray Hill. They signed up a majority of the company's workers and applied for certification before the Quebec Labour Relations Board.

A few days before the Board was to render a decision, eight of the organizers were fired. The rest went on strike and in the days that followed a dozen company vehicles were damaged by baseball bats.

The company obtained an injunction against the union.

A short time later a gentleman named Elie Allard stepped out of a Cadillac in front of the Murray Hill depot and announced he represented the "new" union. "The president [Charles Hershorn] has met me on the picket line and is willing to do business with me," he told the strikers and non-strikers. He represented the Canadian Federation of Independent Associations. About 30 men signed cards, and the Teamsters saw their slim majority slip away.

Ten days later, the Labour Relations Board ruled that Murray Hill was outside its jurisdiction because it operated under a federal contract. That was the end of unionism at Murray Hill.

The CFIA is represented by the law firm of Guertin, Gagnon & Lafleur, the same firm that represents Murray Hill.

Eight years later, in 1970, Elie Allard, the gentleman in the Cadillac, turned up as a spokesman for the Association des Employés de l'Industrie du Taxi de Montréal, affiliated with the CFIA. In a press release, the Association claimed it had 10,000 members and called a general meeting at a school hall.

Montreal police visited the MLT's offices the day of the meeting and warned its militants to stay away. That night the school was guarded by members of the police riot squad.

Four taxi drivers showed up.

The MLT never succeeded in organizing Montreal's cabbies, but it still is the principal group lobbying on their behalf. It was largely if not totally responsible for the drivers' partial victory in gaining access to Montreal's International Airport. Still a loose-knit organization, the MLT is informally affiliated with the Montreal Central Council of the CNTU and is a member of the Front Commun de Transport, a grouping of unions involved in Montreal transportation. The Front has had some success in its propaganda campaign against Murray Hill. In July 1972 the company was found guilty of operating charter bus services without the necessary permits for approximately 30 years. The suit was brought against Murray Hill by the Montreal Urban Community Transportation Commission, which was suffering unfair competition in the bus charter business.

But the conviction was a somewhat hollow victory for the MUCTC. Two weeks after the conviction—the result of a two-year court battle—the Quebec National Assembly passed Bill 23, a law reorganizing Montreal transport, despite a strenuous public lobbying effort by the Front Commun and the MLT. The bill, among other things, legalized Murray Hill's charter operations and barred the publicly-owned MUCTC from operating charters.

The new law infuriated the unions and the MLT.

"It shows that nothing has changed," chief MLT

spokesman Gaston Therrien told a demonstration. "It follows the new pattern. As soon as unionized workers win good working conditions in the public service, like the Montreal bus drivers, the government parcels out their work to private contractors who don't have unions. Ultimately, because they can't operate charter buses, the MUCTC may have to lay off some drivers. If they want to continue driving, they'll have to get jobs with companies that have charter buses all to themselves—like Murray Hill. The driver gets his salary cut in half."

During his tape-recorded funeral oration, Germain Archambault told his mourners:

> "For me, it's not a question of violent struggle. That becomes a dogmatism and I'm not dogmatic. I'm a pacifist and we, as conscious people, at least conscious of social problems, must arrive slowly at our conclusions using the same words, the same dialogue and the same daily perceptions as the people, so that they can 'prend conscience.'
>
> "If afterwards, all the people become aware, through a total 'prise de conscience,' of all the abuses of the capitalist regime, there would have to be a revolution of some sort ... and I wouldn't oppose that."

Two of his graveside mourners were soon to apply the lessons and frustrations they learned as MLT militants to the art of revolution. Marc Carbonneau and Jacques Lanctôt gradually withdrew from MLT activities and formed the Libération Cell of the FLQ. It was rather apt that they used a taxi to kidnap James Cross in October 1970.

It was also rather apt that when they did, they remembered the plight of some fellow drivers, the Lapalme boys, former Montreal postal truck drivers who lost their jobs when the government parcelled out their mail truck contracts to small private carriers.

One of the FLQ's principal ransom demands was the reinstatement of the Lapalme boys who had been carrying out a long and bitter fight to win back their jobs.

The saga of "Les gars de Lapalme" ranks alongside the history of the MLT as a story of struggle against governments' preference for cheap, non-union labour.

By October 1970, les gars de Lapalme had already become

a powerful symbol in the eyes of the Quebec left movement. For some, they were the victims of government corruption; in the eyes of militant trade unionists, their case was an issue of the fundamental right of association and preservation of acquired rights; to nationalists, it was an example of Ottawa's insensitivity in dealing with French Canadian workers. Ironically, their undisputed leader was a tough, dedicated Italian immigrant.

When Frank Diterlizzi joined the Montreal postal trucking operation around Christmas 1958, working conditions were pretty much the same as they were during the horse-drawn era. It may sound like an exaggeration but they were, and the same conditions lasted until 1965, when Diterlizzi and his co-workers finally got union accreditation.

At that time, they worked for Rod Service, a company that had held the exclusive Montreal postal trucking contract since 1952. Before that Sénécal Transport held the contract. Before that it was another company, going back to the twenties when they had horse-drawn vehicles. Some of the Lapalme boys served for up to 48 years and they say conditions didn't change any until 1965. Contractors changed, but the employees and conditions remained the same.

In the mid-sixties, the men put in an average 75-hour week. Often they put in 100 hours a week, starting at 5 a.m. and going until almost midnight.

They'd show up with their trucks at 5 a.m. and wait for a load of mail bags, or wait to be sent for a load. Waiting time didn't count on their paycheque. A 100-hour week translated itself into 60 paid hours at, in 1965, $1.67 an hour. There was no such thing as overtime.

Walking past the main post office in Montreal was a hazardous business as trucks came whizzing in and out, driven by drivers anxious to catch a load to avoid costly waiting periods. The trucks themselves were old, crumpled and coughing, like many of the drivers.

In those days, and indeed until 1970 the Montreal trucking contract—worth $3,000,000 a year— was never awarded on the basis of public tender. Mysteriously, the contract was awarded on a yearly basis without bids.

Rod Service was formed in 1952 by an anonymous group of businessmen, with connections in the Liberal government and also in the subsequent Conservative government. Rodrigue Turcotte, an ex-wrestler, was the front man. He was a relative newcomer to the game, but within a few years he had made enough friends and money for himself so that he managed to acquire complete control of Rod Service in 1963 when there was a change of governments.

In the best Horatio Alger tradition, he managed to parlay his Rod Service profits into Rod Air, with a fleet of 15 planes, used mostly to ferry rich Canadian and American businessmen to his private club, Rod Fish and Game. He also formed a company called Rod Transport.

Rodrigue Turcotte was a popular man among cabinet ministers, many of whom enjoyed visits to his private fish and game club near Mont-Laurier where the big attraction was hunting with machine guns from helicopters. In fact, several of the Lapalme boys—brought up to do repairs—swear that two former postmasters general, Jean-Pierre Côté and Azellus Denis, were among the guests at the club.

Back in Montreal, it appeared as if Rodrigue ran the central post office.

According to the veterans, it ran in an atmosphere of general corruption and squalor. In addition to the long hours and meagre pay, the drivers were obliged to keep on the good side of the foremen and dispatchers. This generally meant a fiver or a bottle of whisky on paydays. Since the Rod contract was based on pieces of mail and parcels handled, the drivers had to collaborate on falsification of papers to boost company revenues. Inspectors were bribed, checkers and dispatchers were paid off. "It was all-pervasive," recalled one veteran driver.

Rodrigue, being an ex-wrestler, used to like to horse around with the boys. He'd walk into the garage and see a mechanic bending over an engine. Thwack! A boot in the ass. Sometimes it was a judo chop in the back of the neck. It seems he also liked to drink a lot. "Actually," said Frank Diterlizzi, "he was a bit of a mental case, a sadist. Once he even grabbed Hector Cormier, the Montreal postmaster, and poured a 40-ounce of rye over his head. Cormier had to laugh it off because Rod was the boss."

Rod spent money lavishly and owned property in Miami and Montreal. The contracts came every year, all without the bother of ever once having to go through the trouble of public tenders.

But the drivers, most with little education and glad to have any sort of job, had to work hard to see a little bit of the federal money. Sometimes they had to sleep in their trucks to make the morning shift.

In 1965 a newcomer, Yves Moisan, decided that a union was needed. The men already had a company union, but in its 18 years of existence it had never negotiated a contract.

There had been other attempts to form a union, but all failed. On one occasion, a would-be union organizer was badly beaten and fired. Another effort ended more happily for the would-be organizer, who wound up in the Abitibi region of northwest Quebec owning his own taxi.

Frank Diterlizzi watched impassively. Frank was born in Bari, in the heel of Italy, where his father was a police chief and his uncle a bishop. At the age of 16 he emigrated to work in the coal mines of France. In 1951 he came to Canada; he worked on a farm, and then in the mines in the Abitibi region. He then came to Montreal where he had several jobs, most of them resulting in layoffs. In 1965, at Rod Service, he had had a steady job for almost seven years.

"Moisan," he said, "had more guts than we did. He tried to get the cards signed. That guy woke me up a bit, he gave me the guts to do it. He was fired."

So Diterlizzi took up the card-signing work.

By November 1965, the Rod Service employees' union, affiliated with the CNTU, was certified by the Canadian Labour Relations Board.

Accreditation was one thing, a contract was another.

Long used to near feudal servitude, Rod didn't appreciate the benefits of collective bargaining. The drivers were forced to go on strike for the first collective agreement. Mail service stopped in the city for three days before Rod gave into Ottawa post office pressure. The men gained an immediate 33-cent raise, 35 more in four months plus 10 cents in six months—78 cents in a year! And a 48-hour work week.

In addition, they got a grievance committee. Toadying to the foremen and dispatchers was over. Rod could no longer kick and punch his employees with impunity (an arbitration committee awarded one worker $3,400 for a beating he took; Rod convinced him to take $1,000 plus a couple of trucks).

The Rod workers were ecstatic. Working conditions and wages were actually improving. The union, their union, was getting them somewhere (in the CNTU each company unit is an autonomous union affiliated with the federation).

In the next few years, the union struck briefly twice more and wages and working conditions improved.

Negotiations with Rod were something of a joke. More often than not, he turned up drunk, saying things like "gang de criss, j'vous câlice dans la rue" and "damn union is expensive, damn politicians are expensive."

"He used to complain," said Diterlizzi, "that the government only gave him one-year provisional contracts so it was easier for kickbacks. Yearly negotiations offered more than negotiations every five years."

In the end, Rod sent the union directly to the Ottawa post office to negotiate its contract. Whatever Ottawa was willing to pay, he'd go along with. Trouble was, as things improved the lucrative profits diminished.

On January 17, 1969, the employees worked out a new agreement with Rod and postal authorities, one which gave them a 40-hour work week at $3.25 an hour plus group insurance, paid holidays, seniority and all the normal amenities other unionized workers enjoy. It had been a long haul, and the men more than appreciated the benefits of collective bargaining.

Whereas before they had been divided by the cheapness of their labour, the competition for insecure jobs and the petty corruption, the 450 drivers and mechanics now felt a terrific sense of solidarity. They were proud of what they had done by themselves to improve their lot, they were proud of their union and of their leader Frank Diterlizzi.

In the two years prior to that, there had been two national postal strikes and labour relations within the department had deteriorated. Communications Minister Eric Kierans was determined to revamp the service, and instituted a five-day postal week instead of the old six-day week.

One of the first results, in February, was the dismissal of 111 Rod Service employees, in violation of their month-old agreement.

The Rod boys struck. There followed two months of interminable conflict, minor outbreaks of violence and severe disruption of postal service in Montreal.

Rodrigue Turcotte was fed up. The old easy money wasn't so easy anymore. The union's grievance committee was insisting on safe vehicles and refusing to drive rickety old trucks. New equipment was costly.

Newspapers were once again focusing on the post office's odd exclusive contracting arrangements. Rod decided to abandon the whole affair.

Eric Kierans declared that since Rod could no longer provide the service, its contract was cancelled (the government conveniently arranged for the purchase of his trucks and equipment).

The contract was awarded to G. Lapalme Inc., a company that agreed to accept all the old Rod employees and honor their union contract.

It was a rather strange turn of events. The company didn't exist before the contract was awarded to it. The two Lapalme brothers, Gaston and Guy, respectively president and vice-president of another company called H. Lapalme Transport, had gone to the union and said they could get the postal contract if the union agreed to work with them.

The union agreed, G. Lapalme was formed and the men and equipment were transferred.

G. Lapalme, however, was never anything more than a phantom company. The union ran the postal trucking operations all by itself. There was no management. Paycheques were paid by the Treasury Board through the Royal Bank. When the union got their first pay list, they noticed that Gaston and Guy were each being paid $480 a week. It was an unusual contract.

The workers themselves controlled the delivery system, the schedules, working conditions, etc. Government inspectors checked their time cards every 15 days. Except for the financial end, it was a case of worker self-management.

The company's only real presence was provided by Pierre Breton, who was paid $280 a week as "superintendent." He was usually present from 6 to 8 a.m. before going off to duties connected with the parent company's contracts with the Quebec Liquor Board and the Montreal docks.

Otherwise the Rod boys, now the Lapalme boys, ran the trucking operation through their union. (There never were any paid union officials. Everybody worked on the job.)

But Eric Kierans was still trying to improve the postal

system. One of his obvious targets was the Montreal trucking operation.

It presented several problems. One was the necessity of cleaning up after past sins of government patronage. Another was the problem of a militant CNTU union, which had secured for its members the most advantageous postal trucking contract in Canada. According to a then-secret government document, the authorities feared CLC unions might be forced to adopt a more aggressive stance equal to the CNTU.

They also feared the Lapalme bargaining unit might provide the CNTU with a foothold into the post office and public service (the CNTU still remains effectively barred from the federal civil service).

On December 12, 1969, Kierans presented his plan to 'improve" the operation in Montreal to four new trucking contractors—MH Service, Moses & Duhamel Inc., Menard and Desmarais and H. Lapalme Transport, the parent company of the phantom G. Lapalme. These four companies were to divide up five Montreal-zone contracts.

He advised them to prepare bids based upon pay rates some 50 cents lower than the G. Lapalme contracts.

Each company would have a different labour contract, all with separate expiry dates, according to the post office plan. In addition, attempts would be made to give accreditation to different unions—the CNTU, the QFL and the Canadian Federation of Independent Associations.

The Lapalme boys heard about the five-contract plan when Kierans announced it publicly on February 3. It was to go into effect on April 1, when the Lapalme contract expired.

The men saw it as the perfect plan to bust their union. But worse, there was no guarantee that the Lapalme boys would keep their jobs, for the new contractors would be under no obligation to hire them. Even if they were to hold their jobs, there was no provision to respect their hard-won seniority rights.

The Lapalme men weren't young men. Most of the drivers had put in eight or ten years with the post office. Terms of 25 years were not uncommon, and some had up to 48 years' service. Seniority rights offered these older workers protection against layoffs. Now the men faced loss of these rights as well as of their jobs and their union.

The long battle began.

They started their protest by staging 20-man walkouts.

Kierans announced that, although nothing could be done about keeping their bargaining unit or their seniority or about guaranteeing their jobs, the men would be given "priority" when they applied at manpower offices for their old jobs.

The Montreal *Star* commented editorially: "Mr. Kierans' recognition that there exists a moral commitment to these drivers is commendable. But that commitment should not be something which has to surface annually after the drivers undergo the humiliating process of protesting their potential mistreatment."

The union sought assurances from cabinet ministers Jean Marchand, the former CNTU leader, and Bryce Mackasey about job security. Both promised to help.

But Kierans refused to give guarantees.

The G. Lapalme superintendent intervened on behalf of the men, saying that in the past they had repeatedly made suggestions on how the post office could improve service and save money (no driver had ever suggested that the existing service was perfectly adequate). "We agreed to sit down with them," he said, "and we tried to get someone from the post office in on the meeting. But they refused to talk to the men."

He added that "when we took over the contract from Rod Service, we knew nothing at all about trucking the mail . . . it is our men who helped us out and who are responsible for good service. Now this is the thanks they are getting."

The union suggested a Crown Corporation be formed to run the business. Kierans said "if the government took over delivery it could be more expensive than ever."

The protests escalated. The post office started to hire private truckers to fill in the gaps. Sporadic incidents of violence were reported.

Within three weeks, Kierans was refusing even to speak to Diterlizzi. The issue developed into a test of wills.

Diterlizzi, a chunky 41-year-old with earthy, working-class convictions, asked simply for his men's acquired rights, vowing that they would refuse to submit to arbitrary injustice.

For his part, Kierans, a former president of the Montreal

Stock Exchange, told Toronto's Empire Club that perhaps one day acquired rights of employees would be transferable but "they are not now." This argument failed to impress the workers since they felt they always worked for the post office.

On orders from the post office, the Lapalme company started firing drivers for "non-productivity." An arbitration board ordered them rehired.

Labour Minister Mackasey arranged a truce, but it was broken after an incredible gaffe by Kierans.

On March 16, he offered to buy the men off with an offer of a $350,000 settlement—two weeks' salary for each man, plus one week's salary for every year of service up to 28 years. It amounted to from $260 to $3,640 per man.

The men took it as an insult, saying they only wanted their jobs. The same evening the offer was made, the garages of several private truckers, including Phillips Security Agency, were hit by Molotov cocktails.

After taking a vote the union dismissed the offer, accusing Kierans of union busting through the "same money grubbing tactics he used on St. James Street."

With their backs against the wall and the April 1 deadline approaching, the Lapalme boys' harassment campaign escalated. One day they all showed up for work, loaded their trucks with mail, surrounded the main post office wagon-train fashion, and simply locked the trucks. On days they didn't report for work, dozens of private trucks were run down in the streets of Montreal and smashed up. The main post office asked for police to ride shotgun on the trucks. Sympathy for the workers was strong, however, and the Montreal Police Brotherhood declared that a "policeman's duties don't include strikebreaking." One day all the regular post office tucks in Montreal disappeared; the Lapalme men had loaded them up and driven them all to a vacant lot in the city's East End.

Montreal's postal services were totally disrupted as the conflict dragged on for weeks. The local branches of the Postal Workers Union and the Letter Carriers, both CLC unions, showed their solidarity by refusing to do any work ordinarily performed by the Lapalme men. All other trade union outfits expressed support.

The bitter struggle assumed crisis proportions in the

federal cabinet when Bryce Mackasey threatened to resign if the Lapalme boys failed to get a decent break.

Finally, as the minor guerrilla war continued to flare in Montreal, Prime Minister Trudeau named H. Carl Goldenberg to mediate the dispute. On March 28, three days before the April 1 deadline, Goldenberg issued a report condemning the Kierans plan to issue separate new contracts. He reported that the new scheme was rather odd since none of the new contracting companies existed prior to the awarding of contracts. His report stated "that the companies appear to have been incorporated only after certain individuals who had submitted tenders were advised that their tenders had been accepted."

Since none of the companies was organized and none had posted performance contracts as stipulated by law, he recommended that the new contracts be cancelled. He recommended further that the whole operation be integrated into the post office.

The government acceded and offered to hire 257 of the 457 men full time and another 40 part time. Salaries were to be 25 to 97 cents lower than before. The men were not to be granted any seniority rights, nor were they to be able to keep their bargaining unit.

That meant a 64-year-old driver with 48 years' service could, if he was lucky enough to get his old job, return to work for a year and then retire with all the accumulated benefits of one year's service to the post office.

April 1, midnight, was set as the deadline for acceptance of the offer.

The workers held a meeting in the St-Sauveur Church hall. They were adamant about one thing. They wanted to stick together and keep their union.

CNTU president Marcel Pepin told them: "At stake is your human dignity and your freedom of choice as union men to belong to whatever union you want. You will have to decide whether to crawl before the cruelty of Ottawa or to stand up as the true men you are."

They gave him a five-minute standing ovation.

The feeling of bitterness was running high as Pepin cautioned the men: "There is nothing those people in Ottawa would like to see more than riots in the streets of Montreal or a few murders . . . ."

The government proceeded to hire fleets of trucks to run the mail temporarily as the post office attempted to organize its new service.

The guerrilla war escalated. Squads of angry men disrupted the trucking operation. Daily there were reports of trucks damaged or hijacked, postal substations bombed and mail boxes sabotaged.

Meanwhile the government went through $3,000,000 in its attempt to break the union and set up its own service. It bought 315 old Lapalme trucks plus all the trucks the newly defunct contractors had purchased. In all, the government ended up with 185 trucks too many. By May 8, it had spent $379,090 on security alone.

The guerrilla campaign continued unabated as les gars de Lapalme won increased support for their determined battle. Six months later, on August 14, the toll, according to post office sources, stood at: 662 trucks attacked; 104 postal stations hit; 75 people injured, including one Lapalme man shot by security forces; 102 arrested; 7 dynamite bombings; 1,200 post boxes and 492 relay boxes damaged.

The conflict dragged on all summer and into the fall. By this time the drivers were collecting unemployment insurance plus $25 each from the CNTU. All the money was put into a pot and divided up according to each man's need.

The post office sent personal letters to many of the men offering them jobs. A few accepted, but the great majority refused to break solidarity.

By October, efforts to re-open negotiations had succeeded, this time with the new minister responsible for the post office, Jean-Pierre Côté (who had once enjoyed his visits to Rodrigue Turcotte's private fish and game club), after Kierans's heavy-handed bungling of the Lapalme affair cost him that part of his portfolio.

But on October 5, the Front de Libération du Québec kidnapped James Cross. One of the demands for his release was that the government rehire all the "revolutionary Lapalme drivers."

On October 14, Côté advised Diterlizzi that the government was favourably disposed to settling the long-drawn-out dispute, but it would have to wait until the whole Cross-Laporte affair was brought to an end.

In mid-December, the Trudeau government made its

"final offer" to the Lapalme men:109 men would be rehired immediately in the post office, another 100 would be rehired within a year, and there would be job retraining for the rest. This meant a total loss of seniority and the loss of their own grievance committee bargaining unit.

By secret ballot, the men voted 88 per cent against the "final offer." They opted to continue their daily demonstration on Parliament Hill.

On January 13, 1971, Côté said the Lapalme case was closed.

February 2 was a typically cold winter day in Ottawa, as 200-odd unemployed truck drivers trudged up Parliament Hill. Every weekday, all winter long, they made the trek from Montreal.

It was a particularly cold, tough winter. They were mostly married men—average age 40 or 45—and they had been out of jobs for one year. They clapped their mitted hands for warmth, placards tightly held in the crook of their arms, tuques pulled down over their ears, faded uniform jackets zippered up to the neck.

Their daily vigil was near an end and the cold wind was getting to them when the Prime Minister of Canada scurried out of the building past them, into his heated, chauffeur-driven Cadillac.

"On veut nos jobs," they shouted. That's what they were there for. "On veut nos jobs." Some of the men started to boo.

The Prime Minister pressed the button that lowered the window of the Cadillac, put his thumb to his nose and gave them a two-handed little boy's nanya-nananya — "Mangez tous d'la marde." Eat shit, he shouted as his car drove off to 24 Sussex Drive.

A week later the Lapalme boys decided the CNTU wasn't using enough pressure on Ottawa, that the labour central's enthusiasm for continuing the fight was lagging. They occupied the CNTU's main offices and evicted all staff workers, including Marcel Pepin.

What followed was one week of acute embarrassment for the CNTU, as Frank Diterlizzi and his men denounced the trade-union establishment—"the capitalist system and the union system."

"All we want," he said, "is a part of the Just Society, not

all of it, just a little part. We're simple blue-collar workers. It's up to Trudeau to judge who's responsible for this whole conflict. It's Eric Kierans, the arrogant millionaire. Trudeau says 'we can't let you win, it would be unfair to Mr. Kierans, to Mr. Drury, Mr. Marchand or whoever.' They've all been dealing with us—the cream of the Federal cabinet.

"They negotiated with me, and they tried, I denounced them publicly, they tried to buy me off. We're not politicians. We're not asking to be senators ... we want to remain truck drivers, we want the acquired rights we won in the past. Every time we negotiated in the past, the government was present, and they forced the private companies to respect our seniority. We don't want to come in at the bottom of the list of 27,000 civil service employees.

"They have destroyed us materially, but the honesty and the courage of 352 remaining ex-employees of Lapalme, no one can buy that or break us . . . ."

He accused the CNTU leaders of playing petty politics, of allowing the larger conflict between Trudeau and Pepin, between the Federal government and the CNTU, to come in the way of a settlement.

The occupation came to an end when the CNTU promised more vigorous support. Pepin went to see Trudeau again, but little came of it.

The Lapalme boys continued their daily meetings at the Paul Sauvé arena and their treks to Ottawa. By this time, their communal style of survival had been well-established. Men were organized in work groups, some to repair cars, some to fix up homes and apartments, others to make cigarettes, others to fetch fresh vegetables in the countryside.

After their unemployment insurance benefits dried up, the CNTU instituted a special membership assessment to provide single men with $50 a week, married men with $70.

But by July 9, 1971, the CNTU executive decided they had had enough of the struggle. They sent secretary-general Raymond Parent to the Paul Sauvé arena with an ultimatum: accept the jobs offered in any department of the civil service; drop the union; take government offers of retraining programs (in Quebec retraining program graduates rarely find employment); in other words admit defeat, or else the CNTU would drop all support.

The atmosphere in the hall was grim and tense.

Diterlizzi spoke for the men: "We, a little bunch of nit-wits, grovelling slaves, we're going to accept an offer from the CNTU that comes from Ottawa? No . . . Never."

"Vous allez fighter," he told the executive's representative. "Vous allez travailler pour nous, vous allez faire votre job."

They took a secret vote and the ultimatum was rejected by a 92.3 per-cent vote. Two weeks later, the CNTU's ruling 150-member Confederal Council met in Quebec City to make the final decision on the fate of "les gars de Lapalme."

As the council met, Frank Diterlizzi walked into the hall at the head of his boys.

"Messieurs les Juges. Here are the men you're going to judge. Make your judgment in front of them."

Les gars de Lapalme stood silent, with their heads up.

The Council voted to continue support and press forward with a new fall offensive to seek a just settlement.

The Lapalme boys kept marching, not only in Ottawa but in towns and cities around Quebec alongside local union supporters. They managed to stay in the news. It seemed they'd never go away.

Early in September 1971, Radio-Canada, the increasingly tame French half of the CBC, issued an edict banning the use on air of the term "les gars de Lapalme." The term, the edict said, carries "a popular, vulgar and political connotation."

All through the fall and winter, they kept up their fight, as the CNTU poured two million dollars into the cause. The sheer cost started taking its toll.

By the spring of 1972, a new element crept into the Lapalme affair. Sharp political divisions were beginning to emerge within the CNTU as left and right wings prepared for the union central's annual convention in June. It was apparent that the left was going to overwhelm the convention and win all important executive positions.

The right, led by vice-president Paul-Emile Dalpé, attempted a divisive tactic by leaking word to the press that some of the Lapalme boys were defrauding the CNTU of money earmarked for their support. It was assumed that the charge would hurt the left, which furnished the most enthusiastic support for the Lapalme struggle.

In the ensuing controversy, an inquiry uncovered evidence that there was unsatisfactory accounting for some $20,000 earmarked for the Lapalme boys. Although nothing was proved, and it was impossible to determine just what, if anything, had been done, it appeared that the willingness to continue financial support was evaporating.

At the convention, the director of the CNTU's political action program, André l'Heureux, a left-winger and longtime advocate of the drivers' seemingly lost cause, delivered a report saying just that—the fight was lost. He recommended that the CNTU discontinue financial support and instead direct its efforts to obtaining jobs for the men.

However, Michel Chartrand and others fought the report on the convention floor. When a vote was taken, a narrow majority opted in favour of les gars de Lapalme. After more than two years of costly struggle, the 150 or so remaining Lapalme boys were still marching.

III

October 1970:
The Santo Domingo of Pierre Elliott Trudeau

For Montreal, accustomed over the last few years to rushing mass demonstrations in the streets, gunfights at the Murray Hill garage, police strikes, student strikes and occupations, 1970 seemed to be singularly quiet.*

The most significant political event was the April 29 election, in which the liberal-separatist Parti Québécois of René Lévesque won one quarter of the popular vote and a tenth of the National Assembly's seats.

Much of the organized left was in disarray; the rest of it was working either in the Parti Québécois or with citizens' committees. The rise of citizens' committees and the left's shedding of its student image to work in clinics and with labour unions, reflected the peaceful form political activity was taking.

Premier Bourassa was planning a visit to the U.S. to make his first major plea for American investment, a plea based on the argument that Quebec was stable. In Ottawa, Prime Minister Trudeau was preparing a Speech from the Throne that stressed his confidence in the state of the Canadian confederation. Pollution was the main item on the federal agenda.

Then the balloon burst.

The kidnapping of James Cross from his home on wealthy Redpath Crescent on Monday, October 5, touched off a series of events that left the country reeling. The appearance in court a month later of scores of people charged with offences as amazing as seditious cospiracy to overthrow the government marked what seemed an utter transformation in the fortunes of Quebec and Canada.

In between, the country had experienced a public battle of demands and refusals between the FLQ and the government; the kidnapping of Quebec Labour Minister Pierre Laporte;

*This chapter is based on "The Santo Domingo of Pierre Elliott Trudeau," by Last Post staff, Last Post, November 1970.

the entry of thousands of troops into Montreal and Ottawa; the proclamation of the War Measures Act with its near-dictatorial powers; the discovery of Laporte's body in the trunk of a car after a curious set of events that no one has yet fully explained; the arrest of hundreds of people after at least 2,000 police raids; and a series of statements by high political figures that confused even the most credulous.

On Monday, October 5, a country's hysteria was unleashed, and grew through the weeks. At its peak, in the midst of the rumours about "apprehended insurrections," "coups," and "armed uprisings" that were being cried from Ottawa, one reporter remarked, in the wry wit that sometimes comes out of frightening events, that "This is the first time in this country we've had a counter-revolution before having had a revolution."

The remark doesn't stand the test of cold analysis, but it had a grain of truth in it, and at least it underscored some of the unreality of the events that exploded on the cool morning of October 5.

The central part of the rumours, and the strangest story that blew in the October wind, was of the *coup d'état* that never took place. This supposed plot—or these plots, for the exact details depended on which government spokesman you happened to be listening to—was referred to again and again after the War Measures Act was invoked October 16, and it is worth examining closely.

It appeared in two stages—first as a complex conspiracy by the FLQ and its sympathizers, secondly as an attempt by moderate nationalists to set up a provisional government to supplant the Bourassa cabinet in Quebec City. In a further twist, some, such as Mayor Jean Drapeau, linked the two by saying that the moderates would have opened the way to the revolutionaries.

When the War Measures Act was proclaimed, government ministers painted a vast canvas of revolutions in the offing. "They will stop at nothing to subvert democratic government in this country," Justice Minister John Turner told the House of Commons. "While their prime target today may be the government of Quebec, there is every reason to assume—indeed, I think there are many clear indications—that other governments and indeed the central government of this country fall within the purview of their efforts."

A conspiracy of that scope requires a lot of manpower, and Canadians were assured that the FLQ had it available. The Quebec City newspaper *Le Soleil* spoke to sources high in the provincial government, in the military, and in the three police forces concerned, and reported to its readers even before the War Measures Act was proclaimed that there were at least 3,500 terrorists, armed to the teeth with automatic weapons and 10,000 sticks of dynamite, who were getting ready to fight. Regional Economic Expansion Minister Marchand said much the same thing in the House of Commons when the War Measures Act was announced, although he reduced the number of terrorists to 3,000.

Some details of the plans these thousands of revolutionaries were supposedly following were given by then Defence Minister Donald MacDonald.

According to MacDonald, we were on a "revolutionary timetable," and the kidnappings were part of a "well-known revolutionary formula." In a CTV interview October 25 he said that "on the whole, you had a pattern of incidents here which, given the revolutionary ideology we're talking about, in other situations and in other countries has escalated itself up into a state of disorder in which it will be virtually impossible to carry on the normal processes of government and which would provide, if you like, a situation ripe for revolutionary action."

Another important characteristic of the FLQ was "the fact that they're not organized. If in fact there had been a highly structured organization it would have been even easier for the police to break."

On October 15, however, Montreal police chief Marcel St-Aubin said he was having difficulty investigating the FLQ because of "the internal organization of the movement, as it is divided into numerous small cells." It was St-Aubin's statement, along with covering letters from Mayor Drapeau and Premier Bourassa, that was used in the House of Commons the next day to justify the invocation of the War Measures Act.

According to Nick Auf der Maur, who was arrested under the Act and spent three days inside Quebec Provincial Police cells, the police in their questioning appeared to believe that every demonstration, bombing, and strike that had happened in Quebec in the previous two years was part of the conspiracy. He said they saw the FLQ as being organized along the lines of the Mafia, and they believed that if they could only find Comrade Big the game would be up.

St-Aubin said the kidnappings were "only the beginning" of "seditious and insurrectional activities." But Bourassa the next day said the FLQ had reached the "final stage" of its plan. The first three stages of the plan had already been carried out: violent demonstrations, bombings, and spectacular kidnappings, in that order. "The fourth step—the most important—is selective assassinations." The government had "every reason to believe" the FLQ was now prepared to carry these out. He added that "already" political leaders had received assassination threats.

There were hints at more than this. Federal Justice Minister John Turner said October 21 that "it might not ever be possible to disclose to the public the information on which the government made its decision."

Prime Minister Trudeau, however, said in the House October 26 that "the facts on which we did act are known to the people of Canada and indeed to this House." When Opposition Leader Stanfield immediately pointed out the apparent discrepancy between Trudeau's statement and Turner's, the Prime Minister said there was in fact no discrepancy. There may be information, he said, that the public doesn't know. But that is irrelevant, since the *known* information was what the government had acted upon.

Perhaps the fullest exposition of the conspiracy theory came from Jean Marchand, once a prominent Quebec labour leader, and in 1970 not only the minister of regional economic expansion in the Trudeau cabinet, but also the man charged with keeping an eye on his five million restless countrymen who live in Canada's second-largest province.

"Those who are well protected behind the Rockies or even in the centre of Toronto don't know what is happening in Quebec right now," declared the Quebec expert in the House of Commons a few hours after the War Measures Act had been signed. There were conspirators who had "infiltrated all the vital places of the province of Quebec, in all the key posts where important decisions are taken." There were at least two tons of dynamite, detonators and electric circuits for setting off bombs, thousands of rifles and machine guns, and bombs. "For whoever knows the FLQ right now," said the shuddering expert, "whoever knows this organization well cannot do otherwise than recognize that the provincial state of Quebec and the federal state are really in danger in Canada."

As the startled members of the House of Commons soaked this up, Marchand perorated: "If we had not acted today, and if, in a month or a year separation had come about, I know very well what would have been said in this House: 'What sort of government is this? You had all the information in your hands and you could have used emergency powers and you did not do it. It's a government of incompetent people.'"

Just to make sure that the people who lived behind the Rockies, well protected from the fanatics of French Canada, knew what was going on, Marchand restated and even elaborated his claims on a British Columbia hot-line show a week after the government had struck. He had a new sensation to offer: the Front d'Action Politique (FRAP), the main opposition party in Montreal's civic election, only days away, was a front for the FLQ (whose membership had now shrunk to "between 1,000 and 3,000"). There were to be explosions, more kidnappings, perhaps assassinations on election day. Anarchy was then to spread first through the province, then through the nation. Thrones were to topple as the conspiracy leap-frogged across the continent.

Most of these scenarios were "revealed" in the days immediately following the proclamation of the War Measures Act. Then the emphasis shifted to the alleged provisional-government plot in which such names as Claude Ryan and René Lévesque were dangled before the public. Afterwards, however, not much was heard of these immense plots, and for a very good reason.

In one of its communiqués, dated November 2, the FLQ itself ridiculed the idea of an immediate overthrow of the government: when the revolution does come, it "won't be carried out by a hundred people, as the authorities want people to believe, but by all the people of Quebec . . . The FLQ will leave coups d'etat to the three governments in office, because they seem to be past masters in that field."

That no vast conspiracy ever existed was borne out by

testimony at the inquests and trials that followed the crisis. At the time Cross was kidnapped, said Mme Rosa Rose, mother of two of the accused murderers of Pierre Laporte, at the inquest into Laporte's death, her sons Paul and Jacques were travelling through Texas with Francis Simard. The first they heard of the abduction was a radio broadcast, after which they had to journey across the United States, driving twenty-four hours a day, before they could get to the scene of the supposed conspiracy.

Nor were the authorities able to back their claims that 3,000 or so terrorists were ready to hit the streets. Even with the awesome power of the War Measures Act, with its licence to search, seize and arrest on no stronger grounds than mere suspicion, and with so many raids that, after 2,000, even the most conscientious reporters lost count, the police could come up with only some four hundred captives. Fewer than one hundred of those were charged.

There were some who doubted whether this handful of people could have placed the established order in Canada in grave danger. But the police did not appear to be trying very hard to find out. According to Auf der Maur, Robert Lemieux, the lawyer who had acted as negotiator for the FLQ, was questioned for a total of two minutes during the first eight days of his imprisonment. Pierre Vallières, a leader of the 1966 FLQ, was also questioned for two minutes in those eight days. Charles Gagnon, another leader of the 1966 FLQ, was not questioned at all.

Still the government now chose to spread scare stories about a sudden revolutionary upheaval, a notion it had repeatedly dismissed in the past. In 1969, Montreal's Drapeau administration had journeyed to Ottawa for the government's investigation into the activities of the Company of Young Canadians. Piles of captured documents were produced to demonstrate that a far-ranging conspiracy was on the move. It was repeatedly noted at the time that, while the documents showed lots of smoke, it was difficult to find any fire. Beyond the well-known fact that FLQ cells existed, and might carry out isolated, anarchistic acts, the rest was vapour. The Drapeau administration's evidence had been laughed out of town.

Two previous, abortive attempts (according to the police) at kidnapping people in high places, including the American consul-general in Montreal, had been taken with equanimity. And so, indeed, had the kidnapping of James Cross; there had been no indication in the first week of the crisis that upholders of the status quo had better nerve themselves for the crunch.

Nor did even the second kidnapping, that of Pierre Laporte, bring about sudden fears of insurrection. It was only on October 16 that the government chose to unleash the vast conspiracy theory and to give credence to a picture of the FLQ that could not be believed by anyone who had any knowledge of the situation in Quebec, that it could not have believed itself, but that might conceivably be widely believed in English Canada since the government and the police were the only source of information.

One clue to the government's thinking came from Jean Marchand's Vancouver interview, for it contained more than the accusations that made the headlines. (Reaction to his statement about FRAP was so adverse that Prime Minister Trudeau had to dissociate himself from it the next day, and Marchand himself had to back off.) Marchand made some other statements in that interview that were a lot more significant. Having averred that there were between 1,000 and 3,000 members in the FLQ, Marchand said:

"Now all members of the FLQ are not terrorists. But there are enough to create a lot of trouble and a lot of killing and this is what we are trying to prevent."

Not all FLQ members were terrorists!

Then what were they?

Who was the FLQ?

Or, more to the point: *Who wasn't?*

If not all members of the FLQ were carrying arms, planning assassinations and stashing bombs, what were they doing? Organizing in the labour unions, perhaps. Organizing demonstrations, or working with FRAP and the Parti Québécois.

Maybe if you were a leftist or a Péquiste, you were in effect FLQ. The net was suddenly a little wider, and out for more fish, than we had been led to believe from the impression that the government was just hunting two or three kidnapping cells.

Was Marchand saying that the FLQ was everyone who

was working for a socialist or independent Quebec?

He said: "How in a society like ours can such a movement like the FLQ flourish? You knew a year ago, two years ago or even five years ago that there were FLQ members. *But as long as they do not recourse to violence, under which law can you do anything?*" (None, Mr. Marchand. If they do not resort to violence they are not violating the Criminal Code.)

Perhaps exactly what Marchand was saying was that we need laws by which the government can arrest and prosecute those who follow their political aims even by peaceful means. This seemed incredible, until he made the point that "It is not the *individual action* we are worried about now. It's this *vast organization supported by other bona fide organizations who are supporting, indirectly at least,* the FLQ."

Marchand was not worried about the kidnappers, but about the people who *"do not recourse to violence."* People—by now it was a "vast organization"—who were supported by bona fide groups.

Marchand referred to "many important institutions in Quebec" that had been "infiltrated" by this strange breed of nonviolent FLQers.

With so many people, in so many areas and institutions, it would be pretty hard to ferret them out. Especially if they lacked the decency to commit a criminal act and facilitate the government's job of destroying them.

Most distressing of all was Marchand's statement of the aims of the government:

"Well, if it had been an isolated case of kidnapping I don't think we would have been justified in invoking the War Measures Act because there the Criminal Code would have been enough to try and get those men and punish them. But there is a whole organization and *we have no instrument,* no instrument to get those people and question them."

By Marchand's logic, then:

There was a vast conspiracy of people numbering from 1,000 to 3,000. They were not all terrorists; in fact some held highly respectable and critical positions, and some had the protection of other bona fide groups.

They had to be rooted out.

The Criminal Code permits us to root out kidnappers and killers, but not people who commit no crimes.

Therefore we needed an "instrument" by which we could

go after those people who committed no crimes, and it was not simply a question of kidnappers.

As far as armed uprisings of one to three thousand people are concerned, the government never believed its own case. It allowed and encouraged the story to spread in order to use it as currency to buy time and public support to keep the War Measures Act in force.

On the eve of implementing the emergency powers, Trudeau feared he was losing control of the situation in Quebec, of French public opinion, to the nationalists and moderate separatists.

The Prime Minister had grounds for such fears. Contrary to the early statements by both federal and provincial spokesmen, a significant portion of the Quebec population had not recoiled in revulsion at the FLQ's action. Predictably, radical youth, certain labour organizations, and a startling percentage of average citizens were reacting favourably to the content of the FLQ's political analysis, if not to their *modus operandi*. But even while most of the sympathetic repudiated the acts themselves, the FLQ's highwayman élan and the governments' inept responses left many Québécois inwardly pleased.

Whether Trudeau thought that the strange events in Quebec were bringing the province as close as it had ever come to separating can only be speculated upon.

What is very probable, as hints in the Marchand interview might suggest, is that Trudeau saw the opportunity to move decisively against the separatist-nationalist tide in Quebec and set it back years, if not stem it forever.

One of the most significant statements of the motives of the Trudeau government, and the steps by which it arrived at the drastic move it made on October 16, is to be found in a column by Anthony Westell, a Toronto *Star* Ottawa columnist with extremely good sources inside the Liberal cabinet, which appeared the day after the act was invoked.

Writing under the heading "The Agony Behind Trudeau's Decision," Westell examined the basic premises on which Trudeau approaches the situtation in Quebec:

"The answer begins with Trudeau's analysis of the rise of separatism in the past five years. The decline and fall of the Lesage Liberal government, he believes, left a power vacuum which Union Nationale premier Daniel Johnson did not fill because he never took a firm position for federalism. René Lévesque left the Liberals to lead the Parti Québécois into the void, and win almost a quarter of the votes in the election this year."

The Trudeau administration's entire strategy toward Quebec is to make sure that the vacuum of social contradictions and frustrations is never left as open territory to the separatists, and particulary to René Lévesque. The Trudeau government fell over backwards pumping money and organizational talent into the election campaign of new Liberal leader Robert Bourassa, scarcely concealing the influx of everything from top advisers to Trudeau's personal hairdresser to Bourassa's side. The province was saturated with a well-oiled campaign that reeked of money, and no one had any doubts that much, if not most of it came from the federal Liberals.

When the FLQ struck, Westell reported, "Trudeau's instinct was to refuse negotiations or concessions to the terrorists. Nor were there any doves in the federal cabinet."

But he stressed that ". . . Trudeau grew increasingly concerned at the threat to Bourassa's fledgling and inexperienced government posed by the new terrorism."

Initially, the threat came from one specific source—the vacillation of the Quebec cabinet in the face of Laporte's kidnapping five days after Cross's abduction.

Trudeau's strategy of strength depended on Bourassa emerging as the strongman, the pillar of fortitude around which Quebec could rally, the dam that could keep the tides of nationalist and separatist feeling from moving into that dangerous political vacuum of which Westell spoke.

From the outset, it was obvious Bourassa wasn't the man to grab the bull by the horns. A scant 48 hours after the Cross abduction, on Wednesday, October 7, Bourassa left on a long-planned trip to New York to meet financiers to discuss the power development project at James Bay and other investment plans. When asked how he could leave the country at such a time, a Bourassa aide told reporters: "Jérôme [Choquette] is handling everything in Montreal and Sharp in Ottawa."

In Bourassa's mind, the best way to handle the crisis was to continue his efforts at getting those 100,000 jobs promised during the elections. According to Robert McKenzie of the Toronto *Star,* "the Premier was more concerned with the manner in which he could explain the kidnapping to U.S. financiers than with actual developments in Canada."

Here the crux of the entire crisis developed.

It centred around the way public opinion in Quebec was reacting to the kidnapping. Trudeau made at least one tactical error, and one massive political blunder. Those mistakes proved to be the factors destroying his strategy.

Pierre Desrosiers suggested in the weekly Montreal paper *Québec-Presse* an interpretation that was also voiced by Parti Québécois economic expert Jacques Parizeau, and backed up by some reporters in Ottawa. It was this:

Trudeau's initial tactic had been to remain firm, in an effort to force the FLQ's hand. They might have killed Cross: Desrosiers and Parizeau suggested Trudeau was prepared to let that happen, betting public opinion would swing to him out of revulsion. But instead, the FLQ upped the ante. It kidnapped Pierre Laporte. Trudeau's tactic to back the FLQ into a corner had failed.

This unexpected response to Trudeau's immediate strategy, however, would only have been a temporary tactical setback, if Trudeau had not made one critical political error of judgment. He totally misread the climate of public opinion in Quebec.

Westell himself made this point:

"Another minister feared that after the first shock and outrage at the kidnappings, Quebec opinion was being won around to the rationalization that while violence may be wrong, the terrorists were somehow glamorous patriots fighting a noble cause—the same sort of shift of opinion that happened after Charles de Gaulle's 'Vive le Québec Libre' speech in 1967.

"A backbencher close to Trudeau expressed much the same fear more precisely," Westell stated, "when he said that the Quebec media—television, radio, newspapers—were heavily infiltrated by FLQ propagandists and suggested drastic action would be necessary to eventually deal with the problem." By "FLQ propagandists," of course, the backbencher meant journalists who were expressing the sympathy felt by many in Quebec for the goals and principles expressed in the FLQ manifesto.

"A Montreal MP, on the other hand," Westell continued, "told the Liberal caucus Wednesday that the FLQ was appealing dangerously well to real grievances among French Canadians, and that it would not stand for repression."

This "Montreal MP" was Marcel Prud'homme, who was taken aback when he took a poll in his constituency and found that the vast majority of the young supported what the FLQ did, and that the older constituents violently condemned the tactic but frequently expressed some sympathy for the content of the manifesto. Prud'homme communicated these facts to an emergency caucus meeting.

Trudeau himself let slip in the Commons a thought that had been more and more in his mind by now: the media were playing into the hands of the FLQ by giving them too much publicity.

The government was so frazzled by this PR problem that, while the cabinet was planning the emergency regulations, it actually considered press censorship, of which Trudeau was the leading advocate.

Trudeau's aides had initially tried to suppress the publication of the FLQ manifesto in the Quebec papers, one of them arguing for an hour with the editor of the Union Nationale paper *Montréal-Matin*, in vain, against running the text.

"As the week wore on," Westell reported in the Toronto *Star*, "the question as to how to quiet the Quebec media came more frequently into conversations around the government.

"This was because the critical battle was seen as the struggle for public opinion. Would Quebecers rally to law, order and a strong Bourassa government, or drift towards a new 'moderate' position?"

Others arguing in support of this thesis report that Trudeau, when he was unable to prevent the spread of the manifesto in the Quebec press, himself ordered the CBC's French network to broadcast the manifesto, as the FLQ had demanded. They argue that this was a sign of Trudeau's overconfidence that the broadcasting of the manifesto would actually cause Québécois to react *against* its "extreme" language.

State Secretary Gérard Pelletier told reporters the night it was broadcast that he had no worries because it was a "stupid" document. But the most compelling reason for its broadcast was that the police were asking for more time and needed the government to stall.

In any event, on October 8, the manifesto was broadcast over the CBC's French network in Quebec, as demanded by the FLQ, and subsequently published in most of the province's commercial newspapers. Read in a near-montone, the manifesto's effect was far different from what Trudeau had hoped. Its language was simple, the grievances it pointed to were real, and much of it gained wide support.

Its call was not to the barricades or to an immediate overthrow of the state, but to "make your revolution yourselves, in your neighbourhoods, in your work-places. And if you do not make it yourselves, other usurpers, technocrats or others, will replace the handful of cigar-puffers we now know, and everything will have to be done again. You alone can build a free society . . . .

"You alone know your factories, your machines, your hotels, your universities, your unions; do not wait for a miracle organization."

It rejected the electoral process because "the Liberal victory of April 29, 1970 showed clearly that what is called democracy in Quebec is, and always has been, the *democracy* of the rich." The second "democracy" was in English, just as throughout the manifesto phrases like "big boss," "cheap labour," "money-maker" appeared in the language of the people who introduced those concepts to Quebec.

Many of the major grievances of recent years in Quebec were touched on—Bill 63, the language bill entrenching the existence of English schools in Quebec that touched off massive province-wide demonstrations before it was passed in 1969; the electoral map that created the artificially large Liberal victory in April, 1970, and gave the Parti Québécois only seven of 108 seats with 24 per cent of the vote; the Murray Hill Limousine monopolies that aroused Montreal's taxi drivers; the plight of the Lapalme workers, thrown out of their jobs by the federal government; the failure of K.C. Irving to build a promised paper mill at Cabano in the lower St. Lawrence region, which had the townspeople threatening to burn the Irving-owned forests that surround the town; and the closure of the Vickers and Davie shipbuilding plants on two hours' notice, throwing more than a thousand skilled workers into the streets.

Recurring throughout the document were the names of Quebec's most powerful institutions—Noranda Mines, the mining empire that controls large parts of the province's northland; the Iron Ore Company of Canada and Quebec Cartier Mining, subsidiaries of American steel companies that exploit the rich iron ore deposits of northeastern Quebec; Power Corporation, the conglomerate that owns much of Quebec's French-language press and has extensive interests in steamships, road transport, real estate and finance companies; the Roman Catholic Church; Eaton's; Household Finance; St. James Street, the Montreal branch of Wall Street and Bay Street; and Westmount, the opulent Montreal suburb that houses the English elite.

The manifesto emphasized that it is the "big bosses" who must be fought but the FLQ's call extends beyond the very poor: "there are reasons ... for the fact that you, Mr. Bergeron of Visitation Street [in the east-end slums of Montreal], and also you, Mr. Legendre of Laval [a middle-class suburb], who earn $10,000 a year, you do not feel free in our country, Quebec."

On Saturday, October 10, the day the crisis took an entirely different slant, Premier Bourassa was still in New York. Justice Minister Choquette was preparing a response to the FLQ's final deadline, set for six that evening, with a dramatic television showdown.

That morning the Premier was scheduled to fly to Boston, where he was to meet with U.S. Senator Edward Kennedy. Unfortunately, Boston was fogged in. He had his government F-27 turboprop wait four hours at New York's La Guardia Airport in the hope of weather clearing over Boston. The plane made an unseccessful approach at fog-enshrouded Boston Airport before Bourassa finally gave up and headed back to Montreal. The newspaper photograph featuring Bourassa and Kennedy, one that was calculated to strengthen the premier's image in Catholic Quebec, never materialized.

In its stead, the Quebec population was treated to Justice Minister Choquette's negative reply to the FLQ. A few minutes later, the FLQ's Chenier Cell made off with Pierre Laporte and changed everything.

If anything, the kidnap had the effect of increasing the FLQ's stature. It drove home the point that it was no longer a diplomatic problem, better left to Sharp and Choquette. It became a truly Quebec problem and various groups and people were reacting to it.

FRAP, Montreal's union-and-citizen-based civic opposition movement, publicly endorsed the objectives of the manifesto, while rejecting the FLQ's tactics. It added that it could not condemn the violence of the FLQ without condemning the violence of the system, and its statement enumerated a long list of labour and political conflicts. It also noted that the FLQ's terrorism was directed not against wage workers but against the violence of the establishment. However, FRAP said it opted to fight with democratic means.

The executive committees of the Laurentian and Montreal councils of the Confederation of National Trade Unions expressed their unequivocal support of the manifesto.

Montreal Council president Michel Chartrand said the authorities were getting extremely agitated by the possible death of two men but did not seem to be able to summon the same anxiety for thousands of people whose lives were potentially threatened by a walkout of medical specialists.

Later he said, "Who's scared of the FLQ? Are the workers terrorized by the FLQ? Are the students terrorized by the FLQ? The only people who are afraid of the FLQ are those who should be scared—the power elite. So who says the FLQ is terrorizing the population?"

The union-financed weekly *Québec-Presse* editorialized that the FLQ's analysis was "exact," and that the horror of an armed, clandestine movement should be counterpointed to the horror of the better-armed, equally clandestine established authority.

A survey of opinions on hot-line programs on popular French stations in Montreal showed that the vast majority of callers condemned the actual acts of the FLQ, but over 50 per cent supported the spirit of the manifesto.

A CBC interviewer took a survey in front of a French Catholic church after 11 o'clock mass on Sunday, and found that condemnation of the acts was almost universal, but that half the people he talked to expressed sympathy for the things said in the FLQ manifesto.

Student newspapers came out in favour of the FLQ, some with grave reservations about the tactics, others not. At the

University of Quebec, virtually the entire student body went on strike in support of the FLQ's aims. About 30 per cent of the faculty walked out too. At the University of Montreal, 1,500 students struck and said they would go into the community to muster backing for the FLQ's goals. Several junior colleges and even some high schools closed down.

But most important was the way the second abduction affected the Quebec government.

The kidnapping of Laporte came close to shattering the Bourassa cabinet and the Liberal caucus. Most Liberal MNAs owed more political friendship to Laporte than to the premier, whose sudden emergence from virtual obscurity had antagonized many. Their instinct, along with the realization that any of them could have found themselves in Laporte's anxious position, was to save the minister's life even if that meant compromising with his kidnappers.

The government split into "hawks" and "doves," and it took several exhausting days and elaborate manoeuvring on both sides before the "hawks," with help from Ottawa and Montreal, were able to browbeat the "doves" into submission.

The hardliners numbered four. Led by Choquette, the others in the group were Finance Minister Raymond Garneau, Tourism Minister Claire Kirkland-Casgrain and Financial Institutions Minister William Tetley. Those who wished to negotiate, in the hope of saving Cross and Laporte, included Bourassa, Health Minister Claude Castonguay and Communications Minister Jean-Paul l'Allier. The rest of the ministers were confused and undecided.

"At the start," admitted Choquette in an interview November 3, "not everybody was at the same point. There was a different way of seeing things . . . we met Sunday [October 11] for the first time and we had another meeting Monday; another Tuesday and so on."

That Sunday, Bourassa met with leaders of the three opposition parties in his suite at the Queen Elizabeth Hotel. He also had a 10- or 15-minute telephone conversation with René Lévesque.

At least some of those people got the impression that he sincerely wished to negotiate with the FLQ to save the two lives. According to McKenzie of the Toronto *Star*, two of the people who were in the room stated that Bourassa mentioned the War Measures Act but was against its implementation because it would place too much power in federal hands.

Choquette conceded that "it took three days . . . I think it was Wednesday that there was agreement among everybody." He was prepared to split the cabinet publicly by resigning, if he did not get his way, with all the consequences that would follow if the government collapsed under the crisis. At one point his resignation lay on the table, reported Dominique Clift in the Montreal *Star*.

"You know that a cabinet minister, if he is not in accord with a fundamental decision of his government, it is his duty to resign," he explained later. "I mean my conviction was strong and I do not think I could have remained . . . ."

Choquette's threat may have been enough, but still other steps were taken to bring Bourassa and the cabinet into line. It was reliably reported by several journalists, and Westell carried that information, that Trudeau spent several hours on the phone at his Harrington Lake summer home encouraging Bourassa to hold fast and refuse serious negotiations.

Laporte's appeal ("My life is in your hands Robert") and letters sent by Mrs. Laporte to various ministers made the decision more agonizing. The cabinet was on the verge of crumbling.

Marc Lalonde, Trudeau's éminence grise, was rushed to Montreal and later Quebec City to buttress the hard-line position.

In addition, Bourassa was facing extreme pressure from the Drapeau-Saulnier administration in Montreal. Most of the intelligence upon which government decisions were based was provided by the Montreal police force and their go-between, Michel Coté, the city's chief legal counsel. Earlier in the week, the Montreal police had arrested lawyer Robert Lemieux and seized all his confidential legal documents, in defiance of the provincial government. Montreal police were operating independently of the provincial government, while the Drapeau équipe consulted directly with Ottawa.

Bourassa was left with the feeling that he had virtually no control over Quebec's most powerful police force, while being faced with a Trudeau-Drapeau axis that was calling all the shots.

There is evidence that Premier Bourassa sought desperately for a way to escape the trap in which he was caught—a triangular trap set by the Trudeau government in Ottawa, the Drapeau administration in Montreal and the hawks in his own cabinet.

To underscore their position, the Trudeau government called in troops to guard Ottawa and the Parliament buildings. This ostentatious display of military power prompted a reporter to ask Prime Minister Trudeau just how far he was willing to go; would he curb civil liberties?

"Just watch me," he answered.

Bourassa was isolated from the sources of power. If his conciliatory attitude was to prevail, he needed the support of the people.

On Wednesday, October 14, a group of French Canadian moderates, led by René Lévesque and Claude Ryan (whom no one had ever imagined as political allies) along with all of Quebec's top labour leaders, issued an attack on Trudeau's statements, lambasted Ontario Premier John Robarts for shooting his mouth off, and urged the government to release the 23 political prisoners the FLQ wanted transported to Cuba or Algeria. The group criticized "certain outside attitudes . . . which add an atmosphere that had already taken on military overtones—[a situation] which can be blamed on Ottawa."

It was this statement that tipped the balance. Trudeau realized he was losing ground in Quebec, that a floodtide of opposition to Ottawa was rising. The Bourassa government was divided, but a new alliance of nationalists and liberals and separatists and labour threatened to fill the vacuum.

Negotiations with the FLQ were cancelled and federal troops were called into Montreal.

While troops patrolled the streets of the city, about 3,000 students rallied at the Paul Sauvé arena to hear Michel Chartrand, Pierre Vallières, Charles Gagnon and the undisputed hero of the day, Robert Lemieux. Fists raised, they chanted "FLQ. . .FLQ!" just as Ottwa was preparing to make their cry illegal.

While the meeting did have a certain revolutionary tone, the main thrust of it was an appeal for coolheadedness. Pierre Vallières and Michel Chartrand both said that the presence of troops in the city was a "provocation." But the latter, borrowing from his 25 years' experience in trade unionism, said "never strike when the employer wants you to strike." The message was simple: no mass demonstrations, just go about propagating the goals of the movement, building support in a quiet way. This tenor went unnoticed by the press and the governments.

In a Calgary speech on October 20, Liberal MP Patrick Mahoney said that the statement by ten Quebec leaders (the Ryan-Lévesque statement) urging the exchange of 23 prisoners for the kidnap victims prompted the government to invoke the War Measures Act because these statements tended *"to give leadership in the direction of eroding the will to resist FLQ demands."*

Anthony Westell confirmed the motivation:

"Only a few weeks before, Lévesque's separatists had been extremists on the Quebec spectrum. With the emergence of terrorism as the new extreme, the perspective changed. Suddenly Lévesque was appearing with Montreal editor Claude Ryan, a nationalist, on a platform urging peace with the FLQ—a new, moderate centre, as it appeared to some.

"For Trudeau, the moment for decisive action to stop the drift in opinion was rapidly approaching."

In a democratic society, drifts of opinions are supposed to be countered by other opinions. Opinions are legal. But the opinions of Québécois who did not support the FLQ but shared some of the views the FLQ and the left had been voicing for years were apparently not to be tolerated.

Pierre Elliott Trudeau had to suspend democracy. He could not triumph in Quebec by moral leadership or by the reason of his position. He had to suspend the laws of the country and the constitutional rights of citizens to combat a drift in opinion.

On Thursday, October 15, 7,500 federal troops moved into Montreal.

At four in the morning of Friday the 16th the War Measures Act was invoked.

Police forces moved swiftly and a mass round-up was begun.

Any reservations that had been expressed about implementing the War Measures Act were drowned in the public reaction to the murder of Pierre Laporte. Public opinion, nurtured on horrific images of Algerian-like clandestine organizations, was reinforced with the outrage at the murder of Laporte. For a while at least, Trudeau did not have to worry about justifying the incredible War Measures Act. To point out the contradictions in government statements, to suggest that there was not in fact very much evidence for the existence of the much-heralded conspiracy of 3,000 heavily-armed guerrillas in high places, was not only treason to many people, but also disrespect for the dead. No one could even come close to challenging Trudeau's unassailable position of power. Silence became the order of the day.

But it was obvious that as hysteria and revulsion wore off, more intricate and credible justifications would be required for the actions of the Trudeau government, and for the round-up of opposition in Quebec. Especially since for two weeks, the police were arresting everyone except kidnappers.

The Prime Minister claimed the government had already stated the reasons for invoking the Act, although other members of the government said that the real reasons would probably "never be known."

The first stage of justification consisted of dire forebodings of armed terrorist insurrections. This wore thin as the Montreal elections took place in an atmosphere of total calm and no incidents occurred anywhere. The second stage was imminent.

In his rambling victory speech on election night, Mayor Jean Drapeau, who had swept into a fifth term with control of all 52 city council seats, referred to "attempts to set up the provisional government that was to preside over the transfer of consitutional authority to a revolutionary regime."

But Drapeau had been seeing coups under every bed for years, so this still did not send the story hurtling across the front pages.

The next day the Toronto *Star*, in a story by Peter Newman (though it did not bear his by-line), replete with "high Ottawa sources," gave the tale the necessary credibility: a group of Quebec intellectuals were planning to replace the legally-elected government of Premier Bourassa and the federal government invoked the War Measures Act to forestall this coup.

Within two days, the country was made to believe that this was the real justification behind Trudeau's act. These were the facts that could not be told. The *Star* was acting as balloon-flyer for the most powerful people in the Trudeau administration, and the story was a direct leak, if not plant, of the Trudeau cabinet.

Newman's story did not name names of people involved in the supposed provisional government plot, but it was clear he was implicating the "influential Quebecers" who had signed the statement of October 14 calling for an exchange with the FLQ. Claude Ryan and René Lévesque both denied the report Wednesday morning, Ryan in an editorial in *Le Devoir*, Lévesque in his column in *Le Journal de Montréal*.

Ryan strongly denounced the government for playing the game of the deliberate leak. "This is so gross," he said, "that the more one tries to untangle it, the more it appears ridiculous and stupid. I was going to write: malicious. I am not sure of that. Mr. Trudeau and his friends are out to get certain dissidents: I nevertheless don't believe them capable of such baseness. I would rather believe that they were carried away by panic."

The smear campaign was on.

The rumours, spread from the highest circles, were the very opposite of what really happened. The alleged "plot" to overthrow the Bourassa government was in fact a "plot" to save that government. And one of the central figures in the "plot" was Bourassa himself.

A partial explanation of what happened was provided by Dominique Clift in the Montreal *Star* on November 2. "Premier Robert Bourassa himself," Clift wrote, "was at the very centre of the consultations which could have led to the formation of a government of national unity in Quebec, a move which was later misrepresented by Mayor Jean Drapeau and anonymous federal sources as an attempt to create a provisional government sympathetic to the cause of revolution.

"The reasoning in circles close to the premier was that such a government of national unity, taking in representatives from other political parties and other groups, would enhance the authority of the cabinet in facing revolutionary agitation and at the same time ensure its freedom of action against a preponderant federal influence."

Those who would have entered a new cabinet, Clift explained, included René Lévesque, labour leaders Marcel Pepin and Louis Laberge, a Union Nationale representative (this in fact happened with the appointment of former UN labour minister Jean Cournoyer to replace Laporte) and perhaps Claude Ryan.

In an editorial replying to charges that he was involved in a plot to usurp the legally constituted government, Ryan said that on Sunday, October 11, his editorial staff had discussed various options open to the Quebec government. One of the hypotheses worked out was a government of national unity. He then asked Montreal executive committee chairman Lucien Saulnier for his reaction to that hypothesis, along with other possibilities. Ryan also said he had spoken to Bourassa during the crisis.

The attempt to form a government of national unity that could both deal with terrorist activity and maintain Quebec's authority against the urgent encroachments of Ottawa did not get very far. The idea came up in conversation between Bourassa and a friend after federal troops had already entered Montreal, and just hours before the proclamation of the War Measures Act: "I thought of that," Bourassa said, "but it is too late."

Bourassa had also, as Clift reported, "actively encouraged Claude Ryan and René Lévesque, and other people in the public eye, to issue a statement saying that the lives of the two hostages were far more valuable than abstract reasons of state." This was the origin of the Ryan-Lévesque statement of October 14, later used by the rumour mill to blacken the signers' reputations.

For if it was too late for the idea of a coalition government to succeed, it was not too late for the truth to be so distorted that the strange tales of plots and revolutions and insurrections and coups d'état were raised to a new and staggering level.

With the government carefully, almost coyly refusing ro give the public a clear account of what it knew or believed, the cauldron of rumours continued to bubble. It was not until Friday, October 30, that Prime Minister Trudeau provided additional information, and when he did it was in the form of a new sensation. The government, Trudeau said, had had "solid information" all along about an effort to form a provisional regime at the height of the crisis. If the attempt had seemed to have any chance of success, the federal government would have acted to prevent it, Trudeau indicated. "I would be awfully interested," he said, "in somebody trying to replace a legitimate government." Throughout the informal press conference, the prime minister made Claude Ryan his particular target, even pausing at one point to twist Lord Acton's famous dictum that all power corrupts and absolute power corrupts absolutely, by saying, in clear reference to Ryan: "Lack of power corrupts; absolute lack of power corrupts absolutely."

But while Trudeau admitted he had known about the attempt, and said he would have been ready to prevent it if necessary, he made no mention of the fact that the efforts to shore up the divided and weakened Quebec cabinet had been done with the knowledge of the premier of Quebec himself. Nor did he address himself to the fact that, had such efforts succeeded, and a coalition government been installed, this would have been a legal and constitutional step, one that has many precedents (perhaps the best-known being the British National Government in World War II, with Churchill's cabinet representing all parties).

Rather than deal with important questions like these, Mr. Trudeau left the impression that the Quebec government, already menaced by an FLQ "apprehended insurrection," had also been threatened by a second level of plotting, this time not by terrorists but by moderate Quebec nationalists who hoped to stage a coup d'état. A benevolent Ottawa, he implied, had stepped in with the War Measures Act to save the Quebec government from both extremists and moderates.

The effect of the backdoor leaking of the "provisional government" idea extended beyond giving the government more justification for maintaining the War Measures Act. The first wave of coup theories, smearing of FRAP, references to separatism being the natural breeding ground for terrorism, and the arrests of non-terrorist political leaders, labour leaders, intellectuals and journalists had the effect of tarring the left with the brush of the FLQ.

But the "provisional government" rumours, the slurs on a conservative Catholic nationalist like Ryan, labour leaders like Pepin of the CNTU and Laberge of the QFL, René Lévesque and Jacques Parizeau of the PQ (all signatories to the declaration of October 14) were aimed at destroying the credibility of the moderate nationalist centre that Anthony Westell spoke of, and tarring that too with the FLQ brush as (in Drapeau's words) "the provisional government that was to preside over the transfer of constitutional authority to a revolutionary regime."

The campaign against the left and the separatists widened into a campaign against all significant Quebec opposition to the Ottawa government.

On the night of Novemver 8, PQ leader René Lévesque, (whose actions throughout the whole crisis were directed towards providing support for the Bourassa government, and who rarely lapses into the jargon of student leftists) told a cheering public meeting that Trudeau had acted through the crisis like a "fascist manipulator."

He told the crowd of about 1,000 that Jean Marchand, Jean Drapeau and "above all" Pierre Trudeau "profited from the situation in order to get a hold on Quebec so as to transform the Quebec government into a type of puppet with which they could do almost anything.

"It was a manipulation, a systematic manipulation, of the population with this in mind.

"From this point of view, in the precise sense of the word, Pierre Elliott Trudeau conducted himself like a fascist manipulator."

He defined such manipulation as that which ". . . tries its hardest to force to the edges of society all those who don't agree so as to leave a place only for it." The solution to the FLQ, he said, lay in reforms such as better housing and reduced unemployment, not in the repression of all dissent.

The niceties of terminology like "fascist" may or may not be helpful in arriving at an appraisal of Trudeau's motives, but the fact that a liberal moderate like Lévesque, who strongly condemned the FLQ, should voice such a charge was important.

The government's tactic was the tactic of the pre-emptive strike. It was aimed not only at terrorism, or even separatism, but aginst Quebec nationalism of any colour—against the maintenance of any strong national government in Quebec City. At least, that was certainly its effect, as French newspapers in Montreal queried in their editorials: "Where is the Bourassa government?"

McGill University professor and PQ member Daniel Latouche told a McGill teach-in on October 22: "The federal government, Ontario and English Canada will never let Quebec separate even by legal means, even if the Parti Québécois wins the next election. A lot of us thought they would before, but recent events have shown that we cannot expect that."

If this is what the net hauled in, this is what the net was put out to haul in. Marchand's radio statement that it was necessary to ferret out also those who "do not recourse to violence" had become a reality.

To stop a drift in opinion, democratic rights were suspended. To crush a constitutional idea—Quebec nationalism or even separatism—the constitution was in effect suspended.

Like Lyndon Johnson, faced with the prospect of a democratic, left-liberal government in Santo Domingo, Pierre Elliott Trudeau moved in. LBJ had his lists of "known Communists" to justify the invasions. But the New York *Times* found that several of the "known Communists" were in fact dead; others were out of the country; still others were in jail. Trudeau's revelations of conspiracies were of the same order.

The real coup d'etat in October 1970 was carried out by Pierre Elliott Trudeau, who with one stroke effected a vast shift of political power. Trudeau "seized the opportunity of the Cross-Laporte kidnappings," said Parti Québécois economist Jacques Parizeau, to carry out "the inevitable confrontation which had to come sooner or later between Ottawa and Quebec." He set back political dialogue in Canada ten years, even beyond the stage of "What does Quebec want?" to "What kind of people are we dealing with?"

After the initial wave of hysteria had passed, the government moved to consolidate its strategy. The War Measures Act gave way in November to the Public Order (Temporary Measures) Act, which differed from its predecessor only in detail. That lasted for six months, until it was allowed to fade away in the calmer atmosphere of early 1971.

Meanwhile, the government carried the fight to other fronts as well. As early as October 29, 1970, Anthony Westell gave some clues as to how that would be done:

"There will be more private and public support from Ottawa for Premier Robert Bourassa, as the legitimate government of Quebec.

"The federal strength will be advertised in every possible way; the Maple Leaf symbol announced last week is not a foolish gimmick but part of a planned campaign by Information Canada to strengthen the federal image.

"The French-language CBC service will be brought even more closely under control, to exclude any trace of dangerous programming, and ways will be sought to ward off private media, which have been too easily used by FLQ propagandists.

"French Canadian opinion leaders who buckled under FLQ pressures and were willing to compromise will be quietly discredited. Separatist leaders will be pressured, while the public mood is unfavourable, to moderate their positions and stop agitating against Ottawa."

Westell ended by stating Trudeau's objective: ". . . to polarize opinion in Quebec, forcing the choice between nationalism and federalism, a gamble he is confident of winning."

In the short term, Trudeau did win his gamble. His popularity soared, in Quebec and English Canada alike. The organized left in Quebec as it had existed for ten years was dead. Attempts to revive it over the next year came to naught.

But in the long term, he could not maintain his hold on the Quebec government, or on public opinion in the country. Conflicting pressures forced Trudeau and Bourassa onto separate paths. In the summer of 1971, Bourassa rejected a new Canadian constitution that had been elaborately worked out at Victoria, B.C., and relations between the two governments cooled. When Bourassa faced another serious crisis in 1972, support from Ottawa was conspicuously absent.

The political trials that dragged from late 1970 through most of 1971 were marked by the embarrassing lack of substance behind the government's charges. Charges of seditious conspiracy against Michel Chartrand, Robert Lemieux, Charles Gagnon and others either were dropped or failed to stand up in court. Much of the evidence was regarded as humorous even by English Canadian newspaper columnists.

It became respectable to think that the government had "overreacted" in applying the War Measures Act. When federal Solicitor-General Jean-Pierre Goyer made a fleeting attempt early in 1972 to revive the vast conspiracy theory, it was nipped in the bud by—of all people—Jérôme Choquette. Many English Canadians had longer memories for the Official Languages Act and other federal government actions regarded as being unduly kind to Quebec than they did for the ephemeral War Measures Act. Federal measures designed to placate opposition forces in Quebec (from January 1971 to March 1972, Quebec got 54.4 per cent of the money handed out for new industry by the Department of Regional Economic Expansion) were resented in the rest of the country.

Inside Quebec, the basic reasons for the last decade's unrest had not gone away. What Trudeau had done was not so much to smash the opposition as to force it to regroup. It would be a year before this took place. But when the left did resurface, the year's absence only made its new manifestation seem all the more striking.

IV
Michel Chartrand's Thirty-Year Conspiracy

After the October 1970 crisis, an eerie silence descended on the streets of Montreal, as the battle moved inside to the courts.* In one courtroom in east-end Montreal, Paul Rose stood trial for the murder of Pierre Laporte. In another, in the old part of the city, the "Big Five"—Michel Chartrand, Robert Lemieux, Pierre Vallières, Charles Gagnon and Jacques Larue-Langlois—traded insults with Judge Roger Ouimet as their seditious conspiracy trial failed to get beyond the preliminary stages.

The trials were excellent theatre. Paul Rose quickly claimed centre stage as he introduced several innovations to the process of jury selection, but Chartrand's performance remained longest in the memory for it came from a lifetime of experience. Chartrand and Ouimet had been fellow activists in the Action Libérale Nationale, the reform Liberal group of the 1930s that had been one of the founding components of the Union Nationale.

The strange links went further than that. Chartrand had worked with Pierre Elliott Trudeau in the wartime Bloc Populaire, and with Trudeau, Gérard Pelletier and Jean Marchand in the Asbestos and Murdochville strikes. Vallières had succeeded Trudeau and Pelletier as editor of *Cité Libre*. The same forces had shaped the people in power and the people in prison, the hunters and the hunted.

These points are illustrated by the story of Michel Chartrand, told in an article in January 1971 by his wife Simone.

It was in 1940, outside my office at Palestre Nationale of the Jeunesse Etudiante Catholique, that I first met Michel Chartrand. I was standing in the hallway with Alexandrine

*This chapter is based on "When labour leader Michel Chartrand was charged with seditious conspiracy between 1968 and October 1970, he told the court: 'That charge should read since 1938.' This is the story of the thirty-year conspiracy," by Simone Chartrand, *Last Post*, January 1971.

Leduc, who is now the wife of Gérard Pelletier (today State Secretary in the Trudeau government). We were chatting when we heard a door slam with a great clatter down the hall.

"There's only one person who can slam a door like that," said Alex. "That's Michel Chartrand."

He came stomping down the hall.

"You must meet him, Simone," she said. "He's quite extraordinary . . . very virulent and intelligent."

She introduced me—I was 20, he was 23—as Simone Monet, daughter of Judge A. Monet.

"Ah, a judge's daughter, ma jolie bourgeoise," he snorted. "A judge's daughter, you think that's impressive?"

Alex protested mildly, but he went on in that sort of vein, very mocking and very sarcastic.

He had just resigned from the Jeunesse Indépendante Catholique and the Association Catholique de la Jeunesse Canadienne and perhaps that explained his attitude. He struck me as very belligerent, very strong-willed, very interesting.

I didn't realize it at the moment, of course, but Michel was going through a turning point in his life; up until then, he was what you could call a French Canadian Catholic nationalist.

He was the 13th of 14 children, son of Louis Joseph Chartrand, an accountant in the provincial civil service where he worked for 43 years. He was born in Outremont five days before Christmas in 1916. He had a typically Quebec Catholic education and studied under the Marist Fathers and then the Jesuits at Jean-de-Brébeuf College. He entered Ste-Thérèse Seminary, and later, at the age of 16, ended up at the Trappist Monastery in Oka, near Montreal. He stayed with the Trappist monks for two years. It was a cloistered monastery where the monks held a vow of silence. Perhaps this experience accounted for his later volubility.

When he was 18 he left the monastery and got involved with the Jeunesse Indépendante Catholique and the Jeunesses Patriotes and took courses at the University of Montreal under Abbé Lionel Groulx, French Canada's great nationalist historian. Abbé Groulx had a considerable influence on Michel's formation as a nationalist. It was he who wrote: "It is not a question of whether we'll be rich or poor, whether we'll be great or small, it's a question of whether we'll be."

In 1938 Michel became a "colon." At the time, Duplessis's Ministry of Colonization, along with the Association Catholique de la Jeunesse Canadienne, was urging the "Retour à la terre." They sent volunteer "colons" to build roads and establish new settlements in the Quebec interior.

Michel went along with the unemployed, who were sent to open up the Abitibi in northwestern Quebec. These were people from the cities with no idea of rural life.

He saw men die from eating rotten meat and of typhoid fever from drinking polluted water in the Davie River. "It was then," he said later, "that I realized it wasn't the English, nor the Jews that were killing us, but a French Canadian Catholic government called the Union Nationale."

He worked as a lumberjack, but he wasn't very good with an axe. He cut himself in the leg and returned wounded in body and spirit to Montreal.

He prepared a memoir for the ACJC calling for a denunciation of the government's colonization policies, which emphasized agriculture, the parish, the family, the clergy and the old values rather than industrialization. He saw in this the old ultramontane spirit in which the fossilized values of the rural clergy and bourgeoisie colluded with the state to produce retrograde policies instead of modern programs to develop skills and the economy. When they refused to accept his report complete with photos and to make it public, he resigned and stormed out, slamming the door behind him.

The day after I met Michel, I returned to my office—which I shared with Gérard Pelletier and Daniel Johnson (Union Nationale Premier at the time of his death in 1968)—and found wild flowers on my desk. They were from Michel.

After quitting Catholic Action, Michel joined up with the Action Libérale Nationale with Paul Gouin (who later co-founded the Union Nationale) and plunged headlong into politics.

We all saw a lot of Michel after that. He was very active, always going to meetings, conferences, classes—and working as a typographer. Politically he was a nationalist, with progressive inclinations. He was also very religious. It was as much a cultural as a spiritual feeling. But for him, his religiousness wasn't the Vatican or the curés. His was Catholicism as internationalism, a fraternity and communion of people. Nor did he draw a distinction between the temporal and spiritual things of life, as French Canadian society stressed at that time.

Shortly after we first met, he invited me to go to a concert. I accepted and said we could use my family's season tickets. He refused and bought two tickets. I went with my two tickets to meet him at the concert, but he refused to sit in our seats, preferring to sit alone in the seats he bought. We met at intermission and agreed to sit in his seats.

After the concert, I asked if I could drop him off somewhere in my father's car. "Ah, mademoiselle has her father's car," he said mockingly, implying bourgeois decadence.

He insisted on driving. When I asked him if he had a driver's license, he said, "Oh, you're really a judge's daughter. You like legality."

Despite such comments and rude remarks, he was very gallant, very polite. But he had quirks.

Sometimes at a movie he'd jump up after 10 or 15 minutes and say loudly, "This is damned propaganda," and stomp out.

He showed up at my home on Côte Ste-Catherine Road in Outremont on my 21st birthday, accompanying Alex Leduc. He brought me chrysanthemums. He was quite silent for a while, sitting in a corner.

Most of the people there were law students, young men who were going up in the world. A lot of the intellectuals who worked with the Jeunesse Catholique were also there.

Michel had little sympathy towards them and let them know he thought they were all in law to become agents of the status quo. He talked a lot about the status quo then and sounded quite revolutionary. He said things—health, education, the economy—weren't organized for the majority of people, but for a minority. He was quite different from other young men I met at the time. There weren't many like him. He was very profound, very serious. Even his French was very studied, almost pretentious. His syntax was perfect.

He approached my father and told him what he thought about judges. Just like that. He said he wasn't interested in law or being a politician. My father had been a Liberal deputy under Premier Taschereau. He disagreed with Taschereau's policies, but he had nowhere to go. As a compromise he quit and was named a judge. Michel thought he should have battled for his ideas instead of becoming a judge. My father thought this attitude showed Michel to be impractical and incapable of understanding realities. Michel said he was going to stay active in politics but in the opposition. He added he'd probably end up in jail for his ideas.

My father admired his principles and ideals but didn't consider him a good prospect for a son-in-law. He worried about material security and that didn't happen to be one of Michel's preoccupations.

When we decided to get married, three bishops with whom I worked at the ACJC interceded and asked my family to block the marriage. They said Michel wasn't practical, that I would be unhappy and poor with him. My family agreed, but when you're in love you don't take anybody's advice.

Our parish priest at St-Germain d'Outremont refused to marry us, as did another Outremont church. We finally went to Abbé Groulx to ask him to marry us. He liked Michel and said he was courageous, dedicated, religious, but a bit of a fanatic.

I asked him what a fanatic was and he said it was somebody who believed in one idea and put everything, everything into it. I told him that we need men like that, that I thought Christ was a fanatic and that anybody who ever accomplished anything for their country was a fanatic. He agreed to marry us in the Sulpician chapel at Notre Dame Cathedral in February 1942.

The day before the marriage Michel was driving my father's car when he went through a red light. The police stopped us, then wanted to let us go when they found out the car belonged to Judge Monet. Michel insisted he be taken to the station and given a ticket.

"They're not even married yet and it's already started," my mother said when the police phoned.

The next day we had a blizzard. The weather couldn't have been worse. "Le Bon Dieu couldn't give a better sign," my anguished mother commented.

By this time, Michel was deeply involved in politics, especially with the conscription issue. French Canadians had risen up in 1901 to protest the use of Canadian troops to fight for British imperialism in the Boer War. My grandfather, Dominique Monet, resigned from parliament as a Liberal in Sir Wilfrid Laurier's government over Canadian participation in the Boer War. He later became Minister of Public Works in Quebec and afterwards was named judge of the Superior Court.

In 1917 there were riots against conscription because French Canadians didn't see the justice in fighting for an imperial power which controlled Canada. It was a war between imperial powers. The nationalism in those days was directed at securing Canadian autonomy and an end to being a colonial appendage.

When Britain declared war in September 1939, Canada quickly followed its lead. The same issues arose. The War Measures Act was imposed. During the 1940 general election, the Liberals under Mackenzie King promised there would be no conscription. After they won, they changed their minds. The Throne Speech in January 1942 announced a national plebiscite on the conscription issue.

Michel helped to organize the "Non" campaign.

The nationalists of the time, André Laurendeau, François-Albert Angers, Gérard Filion, Jean Drapeau, René Chaloult, Marc Carrière, and many others formed the Ligue pour la Défense du Canada (Michel proposed the name). Even Henri Bourassa came out of retirement to take part.

It was a very hectic time, with rallies and meetings being held continuously. Michel poured all his energies into the campaign.

At the end of it, on April 27, 1942, Quebec voted 75 per cent "Non." The rest of Canada voted differently. Conscription was imposed and the War Measures Act enforced against dissidents. Many were arrested, even the Mayor of Montreal, who spent the rest of the war in an internment camp.

The league prepared to fight the November by-election in Outremont, intended to provide a safe Liberal seat for the Minister of National Defence, Major-General Lafleche. Jean Drapeau, who had just graduated from law school, was chosen as candidate. Michel was his organizer.

That fall, we started seeing Pierre Elliott Trudeau a lot, as he became increasingly active in the campaign. Michel and Pierre were friends, having been school chums, and liked each other although Pierre said he thought Michel a bit unrealistic. He said Michel was a dreamer, a mystic, and wasn't pragmatic enough. Despite his good intentions, he said, Michel would never get anywhere.

There were many meetings to attend and we all worked feverishly. I was five months pregnant at the time, and sometimes the meetings could get pretty rough. Police in plain clothes were at every meeting taking notes, keeping tabs on things.

Gen. Lafleche's meetings, attended by several cabinet ministers and MPs, were particularly tumultuous, since he attracted a large number of young conscripts who had a lot of questions. Unfortunately questions weren't accepted at that time—whether in the church, the family or before authority.

At one meeting, Michel asked Pierre Elliott Trudeau to keep an eye on me, to sort of act as my bodyguard. It was a Liberal election meeting and the conscripts wanted to know why the Liberals went back on their promise of no conscription. Everyone who posed a question was ejected. Pierre became very indignant, and demanded to know how a policeman could push a pregnant woman. He was very gallant, with his cultured language and nice manner, as he came to my defence. He became extremely upset when we were asked in no uncertain terms to leave the hall and were ushered out.

Because of the War Measures Act, the issue of conscription couldn't be discussed openly on the radio and in the press. Pierre said it was intolerable that there couldn't be free discussion, that the police were being used to crush civil liberties.

As we were thrown out, he complained about the state using police force to enforce its power. He was very indignant and upset about the federal Liberal Party, although both our fathers were Liberal militants.

Today, when people in Quebec complain about what the state is doing to people, he knows exactly how it feels. This is what is extraordinary about what he has done. Watch him.

But in those days my husband and he were good friends.

Michel worked for Drapeau but never had the same feeling for him. They were never really friends, didn't share the same temperament or ideas. Drapeau was a right-wing authoritarian in a coalition of nationalists. He used the election as a political platform in a very calculating way. He used to say, quite openly, that he was "a man destined for power." Soon after, he got involved in fighting gambling, prostitution and municipal corruption. But he was only interested in legal cleanups. The necessity for social reform never struck him. He wasn't out to change structures.

During this time, Michel continued to work as replacement typographer, was active in the co-operative movement, and took part in the formation of the Bloc Populaire Candien, of which he was director. (André Laurendeau, who later helped to head the B & B Commission, was secretary-general of the Bloc. The Bloc rallied support against Canada's subordination to Britain in the war.) In addition, Michel took courses at the University of Montreal.

Michel was asked to report to the Jacques Cartier military depot, where he said he was willing to fight for Canada but only on Canadian soil. At any rate he refused to sign his medical examination papers because they were written only in English. When asked what corps he wanted to go in, he replied, "The diplomatic corps." He refused to report a second time. He was never bothered again during the war, except for being arrested once for passing out anti-military leaflets.

It was a very stimulating and active time in our lives. Michel had already developed his rapid, boisterous speaking style, standing up there on the platform with the young lights of the day — Jean Drapeau, now Mayor of Montreal, Trudeau, Marc Carrière, who was arrested and is now head of Dupuis Frères department stores, Gérard Filion, later publisher of *Le Devoir* and now president of Marine Industries in Sorel, Laurendeau and all sorts of people who today are judges, deputy ministers or company directors.

In his book on the conscription crisis, André Laurendeau wrote: "The battle was raging in November. It was a young and bristling audience that they addressed with passion. Michel Chartrand attacked Abbé Sabourin, the military chaplain who had just become a sort of celebrity for his long discourse on the glories of Great Britain. 'I love England because ...' Sabourin had said. I like England, Chartrand responded, but his *becauses* varied from those of the chaplain; all the grievances that we hold against 'Mother England.' He answered in his virulent style, acridly, with a violence that seized us all. The Royal Canadian Mounted Police had representatives in the crowd: Chartrand recognized them, called to them, and repeated certain of his more inflammatory phrases, repeating them slowly so that the journalists present would have time to write them all down. We were all convinced that Chartrand would be arrested . . . ."

Needless to say, Jean Drapeau lost his first election in the fall of 1942 as an anti-conscription candidate in Outremont, one of the few ridings in Quebec to vote in favour of conscription in the earlier referendum.

In the summer of 1943, Michel ran Paul Massé's campaign in Montreal-Cartier in a federal by-election. They lost by 150 votes—to Fred Rose, the only Communist ever to be elected to the House of Commons. (In another by-election Bloc candidate Armand Choquette defeated a Liberal by the name of Louis Stephen St-Laurent.) In the 1944 provincial elections, the Bloc received 16 per cent of the vote and elected three deputies, including Laurendeau. But the Union Nationale and Duplessis won. Michel himself was a candidate.

Once the war was over, the Bloc died and Michel prepared to redirect his energies, this time against the provincial government.

Meanwhile, we had five children in our first five years of marriage and Michel devoted himself to the co-operative movement, typography, and his family. He proved himself to be a very good family man and was much more the educator of the children than I was. Five children in five years might seem a bit exaggerated, but Michel liked children and it never bothered him to get up in the middle of the night to feed them. He was very attentive and helpful. As a result, I never found it too hard.

In the early part of 1949 we were leading a fairly settled life. Michel was still active in things, but he held a steady job and our family was growing. He belonged to the typographers' union (which he considered too tame) but he hadn't been very much involved in union activities, preferring his work in food, housing and savings co-operatives. He even set up a Caisse Populaire.

A strike broke out that year in Asbestos, Quebec, at the Johns-Manville Co., an American-owned mining outfit. The union was trying to get recognition and Premier Maurice Duplessis was determined to crush it, in order to keep his promise of cheap labour and high profits for American capital.

One evening, just after we had finished supper, Gérard Pelletier, who at that time was a reporter for *Le Devoir*, dropped by with Phillippe Gérard, one of the best strike organizers with the old Canadian Catholic Confederation of Labour, the predecessor to the Confederation of National Trade Unions.

They told Michel they were on their way to Asbestos. The strike was going badly, the workers were becoming a bit discouraged. The strike was considered illegal, the police were brutal and the clergy was against the union. They asked Michel to come along and speak to the workers, show them they had outside support.

I told my husband that we now had a family and that perhaps he might lose his job if he got involved in the strike, because in those days employers and authorities took a very dim view of such things. But Pelletier and Gérard didn't have a difficult time convincing Michel he should go. Two days later, Phillippe phoned up and said Michel was in jail. That was his beginning as a union man. He has never looked back since.

When the three of them arrived in Asbestos, they went to a meeting in a church basement. Duplessis police raided the meeting and proceeded to club the strikers, arresting several men. Michel and the others collected bail money and the next day went to court in Sherbrooke to bail them out. While in court a provincial policeman was asked to give an account of what happened.

He proceeded to perjure himself.

Michel was incensed. He recalled that my father, the judge, had once said that police were the greatest perjurers of all.

Michel jumped up and shouted, "You're lying, tell the truth."

The judge asked him to keep quiet, but Michel said the policeman was still lying. That was the beginning of Michel's courtroom manner. The judge found him in contempt of court and sent him to jail for the weekend. When he came home the following week, he was furious—furious at the government for using naked force to crush the workers, furious at the judiciary for playing the Duplessis game, incensed at the system based on violence for the benefit of power and profit.

His employer told him to stay out of the strike. He lost his job and went back to Asbestos.

Michel said, "Before we got married, I told you I would be on the side of the working people, that I was a bit of a fanatic. Yes, I am. I'm a fanatic for the workers, for anyone getting the short end of the stick, for the rest of my life, no matter what the consequences."

The strike quickly became a cause célèbre in Quebec, as the intellectuals rallied behind the union. Archbishop Charbonneau came out for the strikers. (Duplessis quickly arranged for his removal from Quebec.) Trudeau showed up to do a social science research project at Asbestos and helped the cause by writing articles. In the end, the police crushed the strike, smashing picket lines, wrecking the union offices, bringing in truckloads of scabs.

Before his involvement, Michel had been a bit of a theoretician, an active middle-class intellectual sort who read books and made an analysis and went into action on the basis of principle. But this experience changed him. He became much closer to the workers, much more earthy. He even lost his semi-pretentious French and started speaking the language of the workers. He was out of work for five or six months, but he spent his time reading up on unions, on labour organization and ended up working for the Catholic Confederation of Labour. He became involved with the textile workers, the shoe workers, and the clothing workers and was a technical advisor to the Conseil Central in Shawinigan.

Before long, he became an expert strike organizer, putting his talents to work with a clothing strike in Sherbrooke in 1950, Wabasso in Shawinigan in 1952, Louiseville, the same year, and Dupuis Frères, the same year. During this period he was arrested several times. In Shawinigan during one strike he was arrested six times, and again in Trois-Rivières. He negotiated numerous collective agreements, worked on political education committees, unemployment committees, helped out the milk producers in the Montreal region and, of course, he remained active in politics.

The fifties were a time of intense union activity in Quebec.

Trade-union development was behind the rest of North America and Quebec workers had to fight the same battles other workers had won in the thirties, and in some cases before that. At that time, making a strike in Quebec was like making a revolution. It was insubordination, refusal to submit to authority. The newspapers and the clergy didn't call you a socialist or an FLQer, they called you a Communist. And in Catholic Quebec that meant you were going to shoot the priests and rape the nuns. And it wasn't made any easier by Duplessis's iron-fisted, anti-union attitude and his labour relations board, or by the Padlock Law.

During this time Michel was drawn to the CCF where, for the first time really, he met English-speaking Canadians he respected. He used to say, here in the CCF there are people who are really Canadian, not British.

Mme Thérèse Casgrain, who later became a Canadian senator, invited some people over to her house to get them to take part in the CCF on the federal level. At one meeting, Gérard Pelletier, Maurice Sauvé (later Liberal minister of forestry) and Pierre Elliott Trudeau, along with various intellectuals and university types, asked to join up. Michel was the only one who actually took out a card and ran for election.

Trudeau again was the individualist, who refused to join. It was the same way during strikes. He would show up, lend sympathy, and then disappear. Never anything concrete. He was too much an aristocrat to be a democrat, he couldn't work with others.

Michel ran several times for the CCF, and came close to getting elected twice in Lac St-Jean and Lapointe. He tried to interest Trudeau to head the CCF in Quebec. He told him, "You're free, financially independent, you have no wife, no family worries . . . you could head up a clearly radical party, a clearly socialist party . . . ."

Michel counted on Trudeau. He had faith in him. He hoped he would become more involved. Even if he was rich, we used to say, he's still a socialist. At one time we all agreed. We were fighting Duplessis.

One of the most important events of the fifties in Quebec was the Murdochville strike. Michel had just finished the Dupuis Frères strike, and we were due for a 15-day vacation, our first in nine years. The strike coincided with our vacation, but Michel went there straight away and at first spent three weeks in the town. It was a United Steelworkers strike and, because of inter-union rivalry, the Catholic Confederation didn't like him working with them at first.

It was a rough, long-drawn-out strike. The employer, Gaspé Copper, a subsidiary of Noranda Mines, was determined to keep the Steelworkers Union out. They finally did, with the help of scabs and the police.

I went out, as I did in other strikes, and helped with the women's organization. These people were really heroic. There were no other jobs around for the men. It took courage to stand up to the company.

Time and time again over the years, Michel went through this. It's hard to understand exactly what it is unless you get into it yourself, unless you see it for yourself. If I hadn't been there, I wouldn't understand how a man can become violent.

This background made Michel what he is today.

He stayed with the CCF, ending up on the national executive of the CCF. Later, at the founding convention of the NDP, he was one of the principal spokesmen demanding recognition of the French Canadian nation. In the end, he didn't go with the NDP, and helped to found its Quebec offshoot, the Parti Socialiste du Québec.

At the end of the fifties, Jean Marchand tried to have him ousted from the Canadian Catholic Confederation of Labour. He was too radical for them. Marchand actually had him fired twice, but Michel took it to arbitration (Michel helped to organize CCCL employees back in '57). He won both arbitration cases (Pierre Elliott Trudeau was the arbitrator in one case) and was reinstated. Then the Metallurgist Federation of the CCCL, under the chairmanship of Marcel Pepin, passed a resolution condemning him for his public political activities in the CCF. In effect, he was told to quit politics or leave the Federation. He left.

Michel stayed with the PSQ for a while but left union work to run a small printing plant we had established in Longueuil. For several years he stayed in the background, out of public sight, running the printing business. He followed union developments closely, becoming increasingly interested in the construction industry. In Quebec, construction workers are in a fairly poor position and get the least amount of service from their unions.

He was particularly upset about the Turcot Yard affair. In the winter of 1965-66 a highway interchange construction site in Montreal collapsed, burying the workers in wet cement. Seven died. The workers always felt it was the fault of cost-cutting contractors who ignored safety precautions and construction norms to increase profits. Michel always felt it was pretty close to murder, the death of those seven men, if not actually murder. An inquest was held (under Judge Jacques Trahan, who in 1970 presided at the Laporte inquest), which rendered a verdict of accidental death.

Shortly after, Florent Audette, head of the construction workers in Montreal, asked Michel to come back and help the union. He accepted. It wasn't long before they elected him as the Montreal construction workers' representative on the CNTU's Bureau Confédéral, as well as on the Conseil Central in Montreal. In 1968 he was expelled from the Bureau Confédéral because of his position in a complex construction dispute with the CLC's Quebec Federation of Labour. Shortly after, the rank and file in Montreal elected him president of the Conseil Central, a more important post than the one he lost.

Once again he was back in the public eye.

Because Michel believes that collective bargaining is only a small part of a union's duty to defend the interest of the workers, he had to take many political positions, not many of which endeared him to the establishment. In 1969 he was accused of sedition during the Bill 63 affair. The charges were dropped.

In October 1970 he was put in jail again, essentially for the same things he and Trudeau and others were doing 30 years ago. They chose to go on to power. Michel chose to stay in the opposition, to be true to himself and what he's believed in all his life.

The others make the laws. I know what it is because my father was a judge and his father before him was a judge and my only brother is a judge. The law is made by men, but justice is a moral thing.

The jails are made by men, but Michel has always been free in his mind, his spirit, and his soul.

V

October 1971: Labour Comes to the Fore

October is a peculiar month in Quebec. It is perhaps the prettiest time of year.* In the cities, the sun shines a good deal of the time and the air is cool and brisk, while in the countryside, the magnificent autumn colours present the rolling hills and lanes at their best. Even in the farm fields, denuded of their crops, the exposed, plowed earth denotes richness and vitality, not death. Elsewhere, some people may think spring represents the new year, the beginning of life. In Quebec, the beginning is the autumn. It's the preparation for the winter, and in Quebec, life revolves around winter.

October has also assumed an important place in Quebec's contemporary mythology. The very name conjures up images of revolution. Way back in 1837, the year of the Patriotes, it was a bright October day when a local newspaper carried the headline: "The revolution has begun!" October brought revolution to another cold, wintry country in 1917. Back in Quebec, during the early and mid-sixties, October peaked with separatist and nationalist agitation. In 1969, there was the October police strike and the battle of Murray Hill, followed by the mass protests against Bill 63. In 1970, there was the "Crise d'octobre."

October 1971 was the time when the "social question" assumed its proper place beside the "national question"; when the bread-and-butter issues fused with basic ideals of social equality and justice. In the past the movement, or the political opposition forces in the province, were largely based on nationalism. With the *La Presse* affair, the major opposition forces began rooting in the left, incorporating nationalism rather then being based exclusively on it. But more importantly, the movement began developing as a working-class movement, based on working-class as well as national aspirations.

*This chapter is based on "The Trigger Was the *La Presse* Affair," by Nick Auf der Maur, *Last Post*, December 1971.

"It doesn't shock me," said Labour Minister Jean Cournoyer, one of the more candid members of the Bourassa cabinet. "This could have been predicted five years ago. The nationalist movement was due to become class-conscious."

In 1971, the opposition forces coalesced around "l'afaire de *La Presse*." It pitted all of Quebec's organized labour, supported by the progressive movement, against Power Corporation of Canada, one of the greatest financial empires in the country, supported by the established political powers in Montreal and Quebec City.

On the surface, the root of the *La Presse* dispute could be traced to something fairly common in North America—the issue of automation and technological change versus job security.

Management wanted to introduce a highly sophisticated, computerized, cathode-ray printing process, one which, among other things, involved "scanning" of copy and translation into type. Such a process would virtually eliminate a good proportion of a normal newspaper work force.

Nevertheless, the major unions involved entered negotiations fairly confidently. After all, they had had little trouble negotiating their previous *La Presse* contract, and they were also in the process of reasonable agreement with the Montreal *Star*, where similar issues were involved. Talks at the Montreal *Gazette* and *Montréal-Matin*, where a lesser degree of change was involved, were close to settlement.

But in 1971, *La Presse* decided to play tough.

As the legally required negotiation period for each union expired, the newspaper simply locked them out. In July, 321 pressmen, stereotypers, photo-engravers and typographers found themselves on the street.

The unions were bewildered. Management refused to negotiate jointly with them, refused to budge from its original position after six months of fruitless talks. "We couldn't figure the company out," says Dan Gilligan of the pressmen's union. "They didn't seem to want a settlement."

Management's goals soon became apparent. They were out to provoke a strike by the other *La Presse* unions, most of whose contracts weren't due to expire until the new year.

"I don't think they were after us," explained Alan Heritage

of the International Typographers Union, "they wanted the journalists. If we had put up a picket line, we would have been dead because the journalists would have respected it and lost their jobs."

According to one former *La Presse* reporter, Jean de Guise, there was a very conscious feeling among the editorial staff that management "felt it was time *La Presse* returned to being a sedate family newspaper, avoiding controversial subjects." This reflected the thinking in certain circles where there existed a yearning to put a lid on the Quiet Revolution and the accompanying attacks on the status quo.

The unions started to eye the company suspiciously, especially because of its link to Power Corporation.

They had dealt with Power before. It was known as a ruthless bargainer, totally devoted to increased performance (i.e. profits) and prone to union-busting.

The paper was built up around the turn of the century by Trefflé Berthiaume, and remained in family hands until 1967. In that year it was purchased by Paul Desmarais's Trans-Canada Corporation Fund, with the approval of the National Assembly (because it is considered a vital cultural and information organ of the Quebec community, *La Presse* is protected by special legislation).

Less than a year later, Trans-Canada merged with Power Corporation, the holding corporation of the Peter Nesbitt Thompson group. Under the chairmanship of Desmarais, Power grew rapidly. Today it is one of the largest conglomerates in the country. (Power is closely linked with the two other big Canadian conglomerates: it holds a 10 per-cent share in Argus Corporation, the E. P. Taylor holding company, in addition to having intimate financial connections with Canadian Pacific.)

The Desmarais group, through various companies they control, went on a buying spree of newspaper, publishing, film, TV and radio companies.

In addition to *La Presse*, the group controls three other Quebec dailies—*La Tribune* in Sherbrooke, *La Voix de l'Est* in Granby and *Le Nouvelliste* in Trois-Rivières; the Montreal region's three largest weeklies—*Le Petit Journal* (circulation 208,000), *La Patrie* (130,000) and *Photo-Journal* (131,000); two Sunday papers, *Dimanche-Matin* and *Dernière-Heure*; a total of 12 other regional weeklies; and 10 radio and television stations. The group also controls movie houses; one of Montreal's most important film companies, Onyx Films (formerly big in feature films, Onyx in 1971 boasted interesting contracts to make films for the Post Office and the RCMP); plus a new publishing company. It is still dickering for control of anything else available in the media and information industry.

This gives the Power group perhaps the biggest audience in Quebec, at least rivalling that of Radio-Canada, the CBC's French arm.

During a period when "the hearts and minds" of the people are at stake, control of information in Quebec is an extremely important matter. (In the rest of Canada, for example, the CBC enjoys a considerable degree of independence. The same is not true for Radio-Canada, where many of the staff feel it is no better than France's ORTF during de Gaulle's heyday, when overt censorship was the rule.)

Power Corporation is believed to be one of the Liberal Party's main financial backers. Power Corporation secretary Claude Frenette was previously president of the Quebec federal Liberals, maintaining a cosy relationship that has not diminished. Power's relationship with the provincial Liberals is also very close. Several key executives, for example, are always on loan to various departments, including Power assistant vice-president Michel de Grandpré to the Department of Industry and Commerce. No fewer than 10 members of the government's General Council of Industry are tied in with the corporation. Arthur Simard, scion of the pro-Liberal shipbuilding family to which Premier Bourassa is related by marriage, and Paul Martin, Jr., son of the federal Liberal senate leader, are both Power directors.

Keeping in the best tradition of Tory-Grit balance, Desmarais also has good connections within the Union Nationale (now called Unité-Québec), having been a close personal friend of Daniel Johnson (the latter used the corporation's plane while he was premier). Connections with the Tories were facilitated through the late Marcel Faribault, president of Trust Général du Canada, which has links to Power, and once Quebec Conservative leader.

Explaining why Paul Desmarais is a generally unpopular man among certain segments of the Quebec population, the *Financial Post* commented: "It may be due to the widely believed and resented notion that, as one observer put it, 'Desmarais as a prince, deals only with princes,' that is, his dealings with governments are handled directly through Premier Bourassa or Prime Minister Trudeau, depending on the situation, rather than through normal channels."

None of this escaped the attention of the unions.

As the lockout dragged on, *La Presse* managed at first to keep up production of one slimmed-down edition a day through use of managerial personnel and imported scabs, some of them loaned by the Toronto *Globe and Mail*.

Then, often during the cover of night, the company started moving in new equipment. Gradually, the paper beefed up its efficiency and size (under normal conditions, ad-laden mid-week editions often ran to 200 or more pages).

The locked-out men could see their jobs disappearing. They were frustrated and powerless. Tempers began to flare.

During this time, the company was setting up elaborate security precautions, including closed-circuit television and extensive screening of anyone entering the building. Staffers reported technicians installing microphones to monitor conversations between employees.

The locked-out men started a minor harassment campaign, and enlisted the help of the labour centrals to launch a boycott campaign of the newspaper and its advertisers.

Scabs and management kept the presses rolling. The other *La Presse* unions didn't want to fall into the strike trap.

Management issued a series of provocative statements intended to drive wedges between the various unions, including innuendoes about the "domination by American unions" of Quebec labour. When a few windows were broken, signs went up placing the blame on "union bosses in the United States." The company was hoping to cut off nationalist support for the locked-out men and to divide the employees, many of whom, including the journalists, belong to the CNTU, rival of the international unions.

Pent-up frustration exploded in September, when a group of men invaded a private golf and country club and broke up a golf tournament banquet for lower-echelon *La Presse* management.

On another occasion, the locked-out men held a chapel meeting at nearby Notre Dame Church, leaving about 150 locked cars parked around the *La Presse* building and entrances, blocking delivery trucks.

The company got an injunction, forbidding more than eight men at a time (two from each locked-out union) to gather near the building.

As the conflict continued into its third month, there was still no sign of renewed negotiations, as a labour department investigator tried to figure out what the supposed dispute was all about.

In October, the journalists' union issued a statement saying the public was being poorly informed. Censorship had become institutionalized at *La Presse*. Events were not covered, reports were amputated, important stories were relegated to the back pages, controversial developments were ignored, and the news budget had been cut drastically in order to pay for the ever increasing security measures. In addition, a new regular feature in the paper called *SonoPresse*, an elaborate public opinion poll, was denounced as a cheap tool to manipulate the public, with results that were falsified and distorted.

In Quebec City, according to one civil servant, all that was required among various ministry staffs to remove a displeasing first-edition story from the front to the back pages was a phone call to André Bureau, *La Presse* vice-president and head of news services. The same influence, including prominent placing of official statements, applied to other Power media holdings.

By this time, the *La Presse* dispute had become a major issue in the province. Citizens' groups, the Parti Québécois, all of organized labour, and nationalist and left-wing movements had all declared support for what were becoming known as "les gars de *La Presse*." Even the struggling "gars de Lapalme," the out-of-work mail-truck drivers, took up a collection for them.

There seemed little the unions could do. The company held all the cards. (Later, Labour Minister Jean Cournoyer admitted he really couldn't figure out the basis of the conflict, according to the *Financial Post*, but he was fairly sure it wasn't over technology replacing jobs.)

Finally, the unions called for a mass demonstration to show their solidarity. There was little else for them to do.

Abruptly, a few days before the planned demonstration,

La Presse announced it was "temporarily ceasing publication." It immediately began turning its downtown building into a fortress. Huge newspaper rolls were placed at the top of stairways in case of invasion. Lead ingots were placed by windows guarded by Phillips security guards (one *La Presse* director, Jacques Francoeur, also happens to be a director of Phillips).

The company issued ominous hints of impending violence, blaming the unions for numerous outrages and a "wave of violence" which few people had heard about until then. There had been incidents, true, but hardly anything on the scale described. Journalists from other media could only interpret this as a provocation. The stage was being set.

The following day, Mayor Jean Drapeau completed theatrical arrangements when he re-introduced his discredited anti-demonstration bylaw—declared illegal (ultra vires) by the Quebec Superior Court. After a huddle with Premier Bourassa, it was announced that the bylaw was still legal since the decision was under appeal.

The mayor declared the area around the *La Presse* building, about 50 blocks, to be a forbidden zone. (When the benevolent mayor read his statement to the press, several reporters attempted to question him on other matters since it was the first opportunity they had had to talk to him in months. He refused to discuss anything, saying he was the "sole, competent authority" to decide what areas of information the public needed. He cited some sort of mystical alliance between himself and the people.)

The ensuing public controversy focussed province-wide attention on the forthcoming march. Labour leaders said they considered the mayor's ban contained no moral authority and offered themselves for symbolic arrest when the time came.

Four aspects of the *La Presse* affair had made it a hated symbol by the time the demonstration day had arrived: management's seemingly provocative policy of lockouts to break the back of the unions and to fire employees; the presence of Power Corporation; the feeling that there was a power-grab afoot to control information in Quebec in order to stifle the voices of change; and the political intervention of Jean Drapeau to provoke a bloody confrontation that would discredit the unions.

Still, the demonstration leaders hoped to avoid violence by marching down St-Denis Street and turning right along Dorchester, the broad boulevard that was the dividing line between the "free city" and the "forbidden city." There, the crowd could be kept moving and any serious confrontation avoided.

The more than 15,000 people who gathered at St-Louis Square that night were quite different from the crowd usually associated with Montreal demonstrations. The face of the crowd was predominantly worker. Most had never attended any of the big nationalist demonstrations.

Aside from the numerous red-white-and-green Patriote flags, nationalist slogans and placards were noticeable only by their scarceness. More typical placards stated (in French): Capitalism equals unemployment, socialism equals work.

When the long march reached Dorchester, the leaders found their way blocked by several city buses and hundreds of riot police. They had no choice but to continue down St.-Denis towards Viger Square and a sort of two-edged cul-de-sac formed by police barricades on Craig and Gosford streets, right in front of police headquarters. It was a perfect site for a confrontation, and the demonstration hadn't intended to go there.

The trade-union leaders offered themselves for arrest; the police refused. The rear of the crowd pressed forward . . . tension was high . . . placards started to fly through the air . . . small rocks were thrown at the police . . . the police threw them back. People tried to force through the barricades . . . a Patriote truck tried to push through, but stopped after a few feet.

The crowd had been there about 15 minutes when the police charged. It was one of the biggest displays of police power in memory. Clubs flailed away, sometimes sadistically and almost always indiscriminately as the panic-stricken crowd fled. Street battles flared. Hundreds were injured and local hospitals filled to overflowing. At one hospital, injured demonstrators brawled with injured policemen.

When it was over, a girl was dead and the union leaders declared their illusions shattered. The police had behaved as inhuman savages, they said the next day at a press conference. They called them "Drapeau's Gestapo" and "two-legged dogs." They proceeded to read the Montreal Policemen's Brotherhood out of the trade-union movement.

The teachers' leader Yvon Charbonneau saw it as clear proof of the "collusion of the political and economic powers" directed against the working man.

"The population," he said, "has received an accelerated lesson in history."

Never before had the gap between so-called radicals and so-called moderates vanished so quickly in Quebec. Drapeau, Power and the police had helped to make October 1971 one of the most profound and important contemporary turning points in the Quebec historical process.

Organized labour in Quebec emerged from the *La Presse* affair united—in principle and action—as it had never been before. The two major trade-union centrals, the QFL and the CNTU, ended their perennial rivalry, which so often in the past had sapped their energies. Together with the Quebec Teachers Corporation (CEQ—Corporation des Enseignants du Québec), they formed a Common Front. All progressive forces, political groups, unorganized workers, students, unemployed and social welfare recipients were invited to join them in their basic aim—the overthrow of capitalism and the establishment of socialism.

"This is a sacred solidarity," said QFL president Louis Laberge. "Never again will we be divided."

For political purposes, the Common Front was more or less formalized at a mass rally held at the Montreal Forum four days after the *La Presse* demonstration. Some 12,000 to 14,000 people showed up at 24 hours' notice for what proved to be a remarkable show of solidarity.

The meeting was chaired by Michel Chartrand, who until recently had been regarded as the *enfant terrible* of the labour movement by its more sedate leadership. But Louis Laberge was up there with him, along with the president of 70,000 teachers, Yvon Charbonneau, radical lawyer Robert Lemieux and most of Quebec's trade-union leadership.

Together, they all but declared class war.

Speaker after speaker excoriated the federal, provincial and municipal governments, headed by Trudeau, Bourassa and Drapeau. All vowed solidarity in the battle against "the wealthy, propertied capitalists" for "democracy, social and economic justice, liberty and equality."

Referring to the battle against police a few nights earlier, Louis Laberge declared: "We give serious warning to the wealthy and to the established powers that this first victim [Michèle Gauthier, the young girl who died in the demonstration] might be followed by others, but in future the victims won't only be on our side."

Several of the union representatives, notably Normand Cherry of the International Machinists Union at Canadair, admitted that "in the past we have been naive petite bourgeoisie."

He explained that in the past three years, the work force in his plant had been reduced from 10,000 to 2,400. Before the peak of the layoffs, his union had presented the federal government with a detailed study with recommendations to avert layoffs. "They congratulated us for the civilized manner in which we presented our problems . . . we weren't noisy like the 'gars de Lapalme.' But where the hell did that get us. We still haven't heard from them, and now there's 7,000 of us in the street."

When Frank Diterlizzi, the Italian head of "les gars de Lapalme," was introduced, he was greeted by the greatest standing ovation the Forum has witnessed since the days of Maurice "The Rocket" Richard. It lasted for ten minutes: "Ce-n'est-qu'un début, continuons-le com-bat!"

Le Devoir political analyst Jean-Claude Leclerc commented: "The massive demonstration at the Forum marks a very significant if not decisive turning point in the evolution of the forces of opposition in Montreal and, to an extent more difficult to judge, in Quebec as a whole. Under pressure from their members and from militant new generations, the trade union organizations have obstensibly buried their rivalries . . . the leaders, with encouragement from the base, have proclaimed their commitment toward inter-union unity.

"Even more fundamentally, although all the implications have not been understood, there has been an historic coming together of manual workers and other groups of workers, including intellectual workers like journalists and university employees. They no longer want to let themselves be divided for the profit of the rich minority."

Earlier in the month, the CNTU issued a manifesto entitled: *Ne Comptons que sur Nos Propres Moyens* (We can count only on ourselves). Its opening résumé stated succinctly: "American capitalist imperialism has a direct influence on the life of each Québécois. To break out of it, we must first of all understand the function of capitalism which leads to imperialism. Once understood, it is not enough to replace American capitalism with a Quebec capitalism, but to look for something else which can meet the real needs of the population."

The unions in Quebec were starting to become highly militant, and if this had been expected of the CNTU, the radicalization of the QFL appeared as a surprise. Compared to the CNTU, the QFL—the Quebec arm of the Canadian Labour Congress—had always enjoyed the somewhat staid image befitting its ties to George Meany's AFL-CIO in the United States. Rightly or wrongly, international unions were accused of being part of the American domination of Canada. But in the latter part of 1971 Louis Laberge, and the majority of the QFL leadership, rapidly shattered this image.

Laberge, a short, stocky, burly man, came up from the rank and file. Unlike Marcel Pepin, his counterpart at the CNTU who is a university graduate, Laberge started off as a plant worker at Canadair.

Early in 1971 Laberge stated: "I'm a practical guy, not a dreamer. I believe in evolution not revolution... and while I don't agree with the present system, I don't want to destroy it."

At the annual QFL convention held in Montreal at the end of November, he delivered one of the most militant speeches ever made by a modern top-ranking North American trade-union leader. Laberge said Quebec was an oppressed, colonized and violent society based upon profit for the few. Those in power had no compunction about resorting to legitimized violence to crush any movement which threatened profit, power, or privilege.

"Whatever model of society we're looking for," he said, "we now know that the one we have in Quebec, generally in North America, is not made for us. We have examined the political and economic machine which is trying to demolish us, and we have come to the conclusion that there is nothing we can expect from its good will. We now have to fight with the ardour of the original trade-union militants . . . the origins of our roots, when trade unionism's liberating goal was global.

"The worker is not composed of detached pieces. If he is a slum dweller, an exploited consumer, a citizen faced with anti-democratic powers or a tool of production exhausted by an employer and thrown out onto the pavement, he's still the same man; and it's he as a whole that must be liberated."

Laberge made it clear that socialism is the only road to that liberation, saying that in the past the trade-union movement thought this could be accomplished through reforms. Like many other union men who have become radicalized in the past while in Quebec, he emphasized that the old-style co-operative, so-called responsible approach had met a "dead-end."

He emphasized that while this could be considered a "great national battle," working-class solidarity was the first consideration.

If in the past, part of the movement in Quebec sometimes exhibited narrow nationalist attitudes, the new coalition sees English Canadian workers as being in the same boat they are.

While advoacting socialism, the 47-year-old unionist said he couldn't define exactly what kind of socialism he meant, that it was up to the movement. "The definition of all the particulars of the society we want to build is less urgent than the development of a strategy for 'smashing' the present system, a system which does not permit and never will permit all the reforms needed to build a veritable 'just society.' "

In response to those who say "Just exactly what kind of society do you propose, do you want?" Laberge said: "When you're a victim of aggression, you don't delay things by planning the menu for your victory banquet."

In many ways, Laberge typified the radicalization of working-class Québécois. The unrelenting unemployment rate, the continuing poverty and the squelching of natural aspirations resulted in an unprecedented feeling of unrest and frustration in the province.

At the same time, the average Québécois gained new awareness that the region's fantastic natural resources only provide profit for foreign corporations. The constant harping and preaching by successive governments about the need for foreign investments had finally backfired. Liberal administrations, and the Union Nationale before them, constantly extolled the immense benefits of foreign investment, promising, in Laberge's words "the great earthly, Yankee paradise." It didn't work.

Robert Bourassa's well-publicized trips to New York hunting for investment once provoked hope. But, 100,000 lost jobs later, they simply evoked humiliation. For, by January 1, 1972, the time limit on the premier's campaign pledge, roughly half the promised number of jobs had been created—not even enough to keep up with the growth in the labour force.

The unrest was by no means limited to Montreal, traditional hotbed of radical ferment. Increasingly throughout the province in 1970 and 1971, small towns rose in revolt. In Cabano, for instance, in the summer of 1970, the townsfolk blew up bridges and blocked roads leading into a forestry concession owned by K. C. Irving. When the latter failed to provide a promised plant and jobs, they stopped operations by burning his buildings and threatened to do the same to the forest. "The people feel the forest, the natural resources belong to the people," explained the local priest.

In Cadillac, a small town between Val d'Or and Rouyn, three-quarters of the population participated in a week-long highway blockade to stave off the shutdown of "their" molybdenite mine. In Mont-Laurier, the whole town and region spent most of 1971 agitating against wood-plant shutdowns.

In Manneville, 400 miles northwest of Montreal in Abitibi-Témiscamingue, Créditiste country, the townspeople fought with riot police brought in in October 1971 to put down a protest over woodcutting rights.

In Shawinigan (population 42,000), where unemployment is set variously at 10, 13, and 20 per cent, depending on whether one talks to the federal or provincial governments or the unions, there were numerous demonstrations. Other towns and regions which lay claim to jobless rates of 15, 25 and even 40 and 50 per cent also manifested their unhappiness. The feeling prevailed throughout Quebec—from Montreal to the Gaspé, from the Eastern Townships to Chibougamau.

The most discernible political thrust came not from poor workers but from the better-paid and better-educated ones, who were pulling in upwards of $10,000 a year with overtime. These were the workers enjoying the accoutrements of the good life—a new car, a ski-doo, a cottage in the country.

According to union militants, they were victims of the commonly accepted myth that the more Quebec became Americanized, the greater access workers would have to material wealth and well-being. They were employed by the relatively high-technology industries, immune, so they thought, from the insecurity faced by workers in low-paying industries such as textiles, shoe manufacturing and woodcutting. But then they too—petro-chemical workers in Shawinigan, pulp-mill operators in Trois-Rivières and others—were hit with layoffs. Those who escaped started to experience the relatively unfamiliar feeling of insecurity.

In Trois-Rivières, at a mass meeting of well-paid Domtar workers preceeding an expected layoff of 600 men, the workers brandished signs reading "Nous sommes des Domtameros," a reference to Latin-American guerrillas.

"They felt like a lot of other skilled workers in Quebec," explained a CNTU official. "They believed in the North American system. But when the recession came, they were the first to go. Being the last to arrive and the first to go makes you realize things."

The authorities' attempts to stave off crisis, especially Jean Marchand's Regional Economic Expansion plan, have proved to be dismal failures. Nothing is changing, at least not for the better.

At their 1971 annual convention, the QFL released a devastating study of the Regional Expansion program in Quebec. It showed the federal government handing out millions of dollars hand-over-fist in a frenzied and futile effort to create jobs. It demonstrated how some companies could actually shut down operations in one plant, throwing people out of jobs, only to take advantage of free government money to open up a similar plant in another location; how Chemcell Ltd. could get $497,888 to create a total of 15 jobs, while at the same time laying off 421 workers.

The study revealed how the government has in some cases provided firms with 40, 50 and 80 per cent (in one case, 100.4 per cent) of investments without retaining any control or ownership. For example, the government provided CIP-Systems Homemakers with $1,749,200, or 74.6 per cent of the $2,346,000 cost, to launch a new product. It showed how companies with the greatest access to capital elsewhere get the biggest subsidies. In one 18-month period that was studied, involving $57,655,513 and 213 projects, ten companies—all of them American, Anglo-Canadian or Belgian—get more than half ($30,542,604).

The results of all this have been less than impressive, the study said. In fact, it is simply social welfare for corporations, fat and powerful corporations. "It is difficult," wrote the authors, "if not impossible to discern the least semblance of co-ordinated and planned industrial development." The report wondered why private enterprise "needs gifts of public capital" to make a profit when its existence is supposedly justified by the risks it takes.

"This is an example of how the federal government, through only one of its economic policies—subsidies to private enterprise—happily disposes of public funds to support an ideology (liberalism) and an institution (private enterprise) which only accentuate our social and economic problems rather then reduce them," concluded the report.

This harsh attitude to capitalism comes easily in a province where the populace has traditionallly been suspicious of, even hostile to "la haute finance."

At a recent conference of the Canadian Institute of Public Affairs held at the Laurentian resort of Mont-Gabriel, even a semi-establishment type like Pierre Harvey of L'Ecole des Hautes Etudes Commerciales (School for Advanced Commercial Studies) could dismiss capitalism without raising an eyebrow.

"The capitalist system as we know it is a moment in history," he said. "That boat is gone. We shouldn't even try to catch it, we should take the next boat."

According to the Montreal *Star*, the businessmen, academics, professionals and trade unionists in the audience greeted the remarks with friendly applause.

One of the "poor people" invited to participate in such conferences, Jacques Couture of St-Henri, showed the growing sentiment of the province.

"Why don't we try something new?" he asked. "We always blame others for unemployment—the U.S., world conditions, outside pressures. We're in a system which we don't control. Trying to patch up the old system is just tricking the people. Why don't we give ourselves the tools to become the masters? Why not make our government the motor of the economy, and as for me, that government would be the one in Quebec."

The antagonism towards the present economic system even crept into the Liberal Party. (A resolution to nationalize all foreign mining concerns in the province somehow surfaced at the Liberal convention in November.)

Jean-Paul Lefebvre, who had recently resigned as the Federal Liberal Party's Quebec director (and whose left-wing missionary brother was killed in a right-wing coup in Bolivia) praised the CNTU's manifesto. "The left in Quebec," he said, "seems to be off on the road to glory."

Of course, the entire mass membership and individual unions were not united 100 per cent behind the new mood of militancy. But there was sufficient solidarity to carry it beyond the rhetorical stage. In October 1970, for example, the Machinists Union was bitterly against the QFL's militant opposition to the War Measures Act. In October 1971, it was solidly behind Laberge.

Michel Chartrand and Marcel Pepin were traditionally portrayed (not always factually) as being the respective leaders of the CNTU's minority radical wing and the moderate mass. Yet both endorsed the CNTU manifesto, a much more strident document than, say, the NDP's Waffle position. Both advocated a general strike to support the *La Presse* workers.

Although union membership was dissatisfied with the current economic situation, it would still take some doing to dislodge politically conservative sentiments. And the organizers realized this.

"It would be illusory to dream of some revolutionary cataclysm," said Laberge. "Some people believe in effect that the collective consciousness of exploitation will unleash an irresistible liberation movement and all we have to do is to let ourselves be carried along with it. I don't believe miracles happen by themselves. We have to organize efficiently, starting with often humble and discreet tasks."

On November 2, 1971, two thousand people, fists raised

silently in the air, crowded inside and outside the church in Ste-Rosalie, a little village near St-Hyacinthe, 45 miles southeast of Montreal.

They had come to bury Michèle Gauthier, the young student at CEGEP Vieux-Montréal who had fallen in the *La Presse* demonstration the previous Friday night. Her pall bearers were Marcel Pepin, president of the Confederation of National Trade Unions, Louis Laberge of the Quebec Federation of Labour, Yvon Charbonneau of the Quebec Teachers Corporation, a student from CEGEP Vieux-Montréal, a member of the Front de Libération des Femmes and a pressman representing the locked-out employees of *La Presse*.

To all of them, and most of the people they represented, Michèle Gauthier was a martyr. She was remembered as an activist in left-wing politics and women's liberation. In a full page IN MEMORIAM in the *Quotidien Populaire*, the locked-out *La Presse* employees' daily paper, her husband Michel declared: "A victim of violence jointly and deliberately planned by the economic powers and the political powers, this frail young woman lost her life because she dared protest peacefully aginst those who treat workers like cattle. I dare to hope that this terrible event will help us understand the necessity of uniting in the face of a more and more oppressive power, and to fight for the ideal which animated Michèle: a Quebec where liberty, justice and equality reign."

When the question of her death was brought up in Quebec's National Assembly, the Liberal caucus greeted it with laughs and hoots of derision and a demand by Party Whip Louis-Philippe Lacroix for an investigation of labour leadership.

For his part, Mayor Jean Drapeau declared: "It's dishonest to say somebody died beacuse of the events Friday night. Nobody died at the demonstration. Madame Gauthier could just as well have lost her life at the Santa Claus parade."

The *La Presse* dispute had become a "cause célèbre," one of those confrontations, ranking with the Asbestos and Murdochville struggles during *La Grande Noirceur* (The Great Darkness), that earn their place in Quebec history.

VI

Spring 1972: The Strike as Political Weapon

"J'pense qu'on s'en va dans la mauvaise direction" ("I think we're going in the wrong direction") this young French Canadian lawyer was saying.* His wife had said the same thing in the morning, his mother-in-law in the afternoon. It was a common expression in Quebec in certain quarters in May 1972.

They were commenting on the direction the labour movement had taken.

The entire family, however, were avid Parti Québécois supporters. They attended a PQ rally at the Montreal Forum May 6 that drew a crowd which would be formidable even in an election year—22,000 people. They contributed heavily, too, to the amount René Lévesque announced that night had been raised by the PQ in public subscriptions in a fund drive in March—a whopping $600,000, or twice the stated objective.

The PQ, in short, is a powerful force in Quebec. Its power is not diminishing. It is probably rising.

So is its conservatism.

The unions and the PQ represent the two basic directions in which Quebec, constantly in motion, is moving. The only other force that has gained anything in Quebec is the far right. A poll taken for Radio-Canada early in 1972 everywhere in Quebec except Montreal Island showed the Créditistes, despite a leadership split, neck and neck with the Liberals at 30 per-cent popularity. Unité-Québec (the new name for the Union Nationale) was disintegrating and the PQ had risen slightly since the election.

In the PQ's first flush in the late 1960s, when René Lévesque was still being called "Quebec's Castro" by the business community, it was assumed that the PQ was running on the

---

*This chapter is based on "The May Revolt Shakes Quebec," by Nick Auf der Maur; "Sept-Iles Revolts," by Malcolm Reid; and "The Year of the Manifestos," by Ralph Surette; *Last Post,* July 1972.

same track as the more progressive elements of the unions. In fact, if there was any division to be conjured with it was that the lethargic workers, satisfied with their union salaries, weren't interested in sacrificing their "standard of living" by flirting with separatism. Louis Laberge was happy being part of the AFL-CIO-CLC international union structure, Marcel Pepin was still a moderate union technocrat, the two labour centrals were bickering with each other, and the business community was spared its illusions.

After the 1970 provincial election, when all of the PQ's seven seats came from dispossessed areas, René Lévesque, feeling both thankful and guilty, announced that the PQ would move to the left "to represent the people who voted for us."

It did not.

The first crunch came during the *La Presse* strike of October 1971 when Lévesque denounced the labour leaders, who had led the October 29 demonstration and personally assaulted police barricades, as a bunch of fanatics. He said he would "rather live in a South American banana republic" than in a Quebec dominated by the "ranting and raving of labour leaders." His blunt statement was prompted by the PQ's phobia of being associated in the voters' minds with anything that smacks of being revolutionary.

He got bouquets even from the English-language media for that. But Robert Burns, a former CNTU lawyer who sits as the PQ member of the National Assembly for Maisonneuve, rebuked Lévesque for failing to support the unions, saying that the "PQ is sometimes little more than a progressive wing of the Liberal Party." Lévesque told Burns to get right out of the party if he didn't like it. Burns was effectively silenced.

Just before the QFL convention in November 1971, the PQ's National Council issued a conciliatory "mini-manifesto" pledging solidarity with labour's goal—the democratic restructuring of the social and economic system. The statement said the party and organizations such as trade unions should be regarded as different and separate but complementary tools needed to pursue this goal.

The conciliatory move could not hide the deepening split. And nowhere was the split more evident than in the economic manifestoes issued by the PQ and the CNTU. The

PQ manifesto is not interested in the socialism and transfer of ownership to the working class advocated by the CNTU document—the famous *Ne comptons que sur nos propres moyens*. Instead, it outlines a program whereby economic independence is to be achieved through strict ownership regulations. It states that independence is a prior condition for this. The burden of repatriating the economy will rest squarely on the half-state, half-private institutions that were set up during the Quiet Revolution of the early 1960s and that are being progressively dismantled by the present-day Liberals as hindrances to unfettered private enterprises—Hydro-Québec, SIDBEC (steel), S O Q U E M (mines), SOQUIP (oil), REXFOR (forestry), and particularly the Société Générale de Financement, the repository for Quebec Pension Plan funds.

The PQ and the unions not only are moving in different directions, but are on a collision course. For at the same time the PQ was demonstrating its power with the May 1972 Montreal Forum rally, the unions were mounting an even more impressive manifestation of their own power—the Common Front strike.

The Common Front of labour was organized to press demands for the very real needs of 210,000 public and parapublic employees. In organizing the Common Front, labour clashed head-on with the very real interests of business. And so, what might have been an ordinary collective bargaining struggle was transformed into a political confrontation with a government pledged to safeguard a system based on profit.

The trade-union movement mounted its confrontation entirely within our democratic and legal structures. It was done within the traditional limits of collective bargaining procedures. But it was done outside the mental and political framework of contemporary North American trade unionism.

The public-service strike was brought to an end only through the use of repressive legislation aimed at the fundamental rights of unionism—rights won through decades of struggle. This legislation was added to the standard use of injunctions, which resulted in the jailing of numerous ordinary people, along with the three leaders of the Common Front—Marcel Pepin of the Confederation of National Trade Unions, Louis Laberge of the Quebec Federation of

Labour, and Yvon Charbonneau of the Teachers Corporation.

Labour's answer to this repression was an unprecedented revolt. Thousands of Québécois workers staged massive walkouts, demonstrations and occupations.

They showed their solidarity as they seized control of towns and radio stations, struck against both private and public enterprise. They expressed their anger at intimidation and the denial of democratic rights, and gave vent to their feelings of hostility towards big business and government.

The Common Front had its origins at the time when the Quebec unions began to cast aside their traditional rivalries and put into practice the lesson that co-operation gets better results than bickering.

Individually, the unions had fought numerous public-service strikes. There were hospital and hydro workers, Liquor Board employees who walked out, teachers who struck, marched and resigned, and who, when they finally got a contract out of the Union Nationale government, found it was time to negotiate the next contract.

By this time, the 900-odd bargaining units had decided that perhaps it would be more efficient to make common cause. They broached the idea to the Union Nationale government, which indicated it would be favourably disposed to negotiating with a common front.

The Common Front was beginning.

By the autumn of 1971, when the *La Presse* affair united the labour centrals as they had never been united before, the Common Front for negotiations with the government already had been settled and the manoeuvring was well underway. The Front represented 210,000 of the 250,000 people directly or indirectly on the government payroll.

The contract reasons for banding together were simple. "The Quebec state," explained one union pamphlet, "under the pretense of public interest, exploits its employees like any other capitalist. It does not hesitate to use the judicial or legislative apparatus to repress the workers' struggle. It uses all possible means to divide the workers, for example negotiating with the weakest sector first, and then imposing those conditions on other sectors. The affiliation of workers in three separate labour federations only helps the state's game."

The opening of Common Front negotiations with the government came at a time when the political consciousness of the unions was developing rapidly. It was the time of *Ne comptons que sur nos propres moyens* and the first expressions of Louis Laberge's newfound radicalism.

In the autumn, Laberge told the QFL's annual convention: "We [have] one common enemy and the unification of all the agents of oppression dictated on our part the fusion of our efforts in a single common front.

"The oppressed represent the immense majority. The sharpened consciousness provoked by the open aggression of the economic and policical system for a number of years has thrown everyone together on the same side."

When the Common Front got together to negotiate for civil servants, teachers, hospital workers, maintenance men, engineers, jail guards and the rest of the public sector, it decided to press demands that would have some social consequence, that would in the long run benefit the rest of the populace. This was to be done, with some modifications, entirely within normal, legal bargaining procedures.

The principal innovation was to be the demand for one central bargaining table. The Front wanted first to negotiate the total amount of money available for salaries, and then decide how to divide it up. Following that, working conditions and job security would be negotiated at separate tables.

The government refused, saying it was tantamount to allowing the unions to negotiate government policy. It insisted on straight sectoral bargaining. This would break up the Front into some 16 or more separate units.

The government's refusal, in addition to weakening the Front's bargaining strength, would limit its ability to press demands containing social consequences. These included equal pay for equal work, regardless of region, sector or sex; an eight-per-cent raise to keep up with the cost of living; job security and a say in working conditions to bring the government bureaucracy and public services closer to the people; and finally, a $100 minimum wage for all workers.

Job security and working conditions were especially important to the teachers, since 5,000 of the 70,000 members were slated to be laid off in September 1972.

The $100 minimum was necessary because some 40,000 of the 210,000 people involved were taking home $70 or less a week. More than half got less than $100. This was the most important demand, since the unions felt it would set a precedent, and help make it the minimum wage in the private sector. The rate was based on the fact that both the Senate Committee on Poverty and the Castonguay Commission on social welfare in Quebec set it as the poverty level for a family with two children.

Public Service Minister Jean-Paul l'Allier argued that many of those making less than $100 were women, and that the government should have to pay only "the average rate for a similar job in private industry."

Marcel Pepin explained that collective bargaining was an instrument of change, and this time around they wanted to change the social order a bit.

"The $100 minimum is a new method of remuneration which the capitalist system cannot accommodate and the government rejects it. The basis for this remuneration should be based not on the needs of the market, but on the human needs of the least favoured workers.

"We want to start from a vital, decent minimum and we want to diminish the gap between the best and the least paid. But the present capitalist system tends to widen this gap."

The government felt that demands that wages be paid according to social needs rather than according to the economic value of labour went far beyond the scope of collective bargaining, and were an attempt to force it to accept union social and economic policies.

But rather than say this in the open, the government simply refused the demand for a central bargaining table. A single table was essential so that weak sectors, such as hospital workers, would share the strength of the group.

For almost a year, until March 1972, negotiations bogged down on this single, elementary point.

The government devoted this time to trying to split the Front, saying that one couldn't possibly find any common ground between teachers and manual labourers.

At one point, the teachers actually pulled out, but then returned.

Teachers president Yvon Charbonneau explained: "The negotiations could bring up the whole question of the capitalist system and unmask it. It would be the tip of the lance, the first blow against the system."

Private enterprise, the unions constantly told their members, was putting enormous pressure on the Bourassa government to resist the $100 minimum.

The government claimed it lacked the financial resources. The fact that so many of its employees would be better off on welfare, along with thousands of others, didn't seem to bother it.

Instead, the Quebec authorities launched a massive propaganda campaign extolling the generosity of its offers. The campaign was led by a well-paid force of recently hired journalists pumping out the government side of the issue to the public. The spent a fortune on a glossy, multi-coloured, 32-page brochure entitled "L'Important," which was inserted in almost every paper in the province. They took out countless newspaper ads aimed at specific groups of workers, always implying they would be better off on their own.

The Common Front's own campaign—and this perhaps was one of its worst mistakes—was more internal, specifically aimed at maintaining solidarity. It revolved around its slogan—*NOUS, le monde ordinaire* (WE, the ordinary people). Perhaps because of financial limitations, the Front didn't fully carry its side of the issue to the public, the recipient of so much government publicity.

With negotiations at an impasse, the Front held a strike vote. On March 9, some 75 per cent voted to reject the government offer of a 4.3 per-cent raise, and gave their approval for a general strike. (Actually, considering inflation, the offer amounted to a net reduction for some workers. Under the guise of "reclassification," the government also wanted to increase working hours for some with no appreciable increase in pay.)

One week later, l'Allier agreed to the Front's demand for a central negotiating table. But the two chief government negotiators, deputy minister Roch Bolduc and Reynalde Langlois, a specially hired lawyer, refused to budge. No ministers attended the negotiations.

The Front called a one-day strike for March 24, but a severe snow storm caused it to be postponed for four days.

When the workers went out on March 28, the government was waiting with injunctions against Hydro-Québec workers and psychiatric and chronic care hospital workers (most were non-medical staff—cleaners, cooks, laundry workers, etc.).

After the one-day strike, Front leaders demanded that l'Allier himself, or somebody who was in a position to bargain genuinely, be present at the talks in Quebec City's Holiday Inn. The result was a 0.4 per-cent upward revision of the wage offer.

The Front, in turn, made a major concession and dropped its demand for an immediate $100 minimum, asking for it only in raises spread over the life of a three-year contract. This amended demand was rejected.

The Common Front decided to go for an all-out, unlimited general strike on April 11.

It agreed to provide essential services. In hospitals, it was left to individual unions to negotiate with local administrations what constituted essential services.

The government immediately slapped injunctions on 61 hospital unions.

The battle for public opinion was shaping up, and the government chose to focus attention on the hospitals where it could most easily turn public opinion against the strike.

"Everything indicates," said a CNTU statement, "that the government felt it could easily count on about 60 hospital administrators (many of whom owed their jobs to patronage) to render essential service negotiations impossible in their institutions and thus prepare the way for injunctions."

Workers at 20 institutions chose to ignore the injunctions, on the grounds that they were unjustified and deprived them of their right to strike as provided in the labour code. They also felt they were intended to divide the Front.

As the strike, the largest in Canadian history, dragged on for several days, the media went about their task of whipping up anti-union hysteria.

The English media, particularly the Montreal *Star* and *Gazette*, were especially prone to this tactic. From the first day, before the strike could possibly have had any effect, the *Gazette* carried wild, emotional, front-page stories about patients being forced to sleep in urine or beside cadavers.

"They could write stories like that about general hospital conditions without a strike," commented one picketer.

In fact, the media campaign became so shrill that on

about the fifth day of the strike, l'Allier himself told a press conference that while it was a difficult situation, there was no emergency. He in particular asked the *Star* and the *Gazette* to keep things in perspective. However, there was no doubt that the effects of the strike were massive. Over 200,000 people were out as government machinery ground to a halt.

Throughout the first several days of the strike, Premier Bourassa dodged the issue and refused to make any statements. At a press conference, l'Allier—who still had not attended any negotiations—said that government would respect the workers' right to strike and not resort to strike-breaking legislation. However, Liberal back-benchers and right-wing cabinet members, led by Finance Minister Raymond Garneau, demanded legislation.

Morale on the picket lines was high. Everywhere in the province, le monde ordinaire marched, picketed and pressed their demands. "Man on the picket line interviews" invariably showed that the strikers were conscious of the political aspect. "The government doesn't represent us," said one court clerk. "It represents Bay Street, St. James Street, Wall Street, but not us. Our union is the only thing that represents us."

The so-called "liberal" element of the government— l'Allier, Social Affairs Minister Castonguay and Labour Minister Cournoyer—seemed intent on waiting the strike out, waiting for public opinion to force the unions to accept the latest offer, and waiting for the financial burden of the strike to crush the poorly paid. But the right-wing element clamoured for an iron fist.

On April 19, the ninth day of the strike, the Quebec judiciary struck the first blow.

On that day, the government had come up with a new offer. Louis Laberge had said, ". . . the offers are not yet close to meeting our objectives. They do not satisfy us but they are the basis for study and we will take a close look at them." At almost the same time he was saying that, 13 workers from the Charles Lemoyne hospital on Montreal's South Shore appeared before Superior Court Judge Georges Pelletier for sentencing for violating injunctions.

The sentences shocked and angered the union movement.

Thirteen union officials, none of them salaried, and most of them amongst the lowest-paid workers in the Common

Front, were sentenced to six months in jail plus personal fines of $5,000 each. In addition, their unions were fined $70,600.

Before the judiciary was through, in the following days, a total of 103 workers were fined a half-million dollars and sentenced to a cumulative 24 years in prison.

"When the law is ignored and the authority of the courts openly defied, there is reason to fear a situation which could degenerate into anarchy," read the judgment.

Judge Pelletier added that if the law permitted him, he would have decertified the unions involved.

Union leaders and rank-and-filers were enraged.

Marcel Pepin noted that Judge Pelletier had been a political appointee, saying, "He became independent when he became a judge I suppose. He used to be a Liberal Party organizer. Is his judgment, because the Liberals are in power, tainted by his past?

"Doctors and police have made illegal strikes, but nobody gets charged. But simple hospital workers making a legal strike are condemned like criminals."

Yvon Charbonneau, the teachers' leader, was furious: "The union movement may have to go into the resistance in the historic sense of the word. The day may come when we will have to drop our pencils and chalk. This government won't compromise except in the face of arms . . . maybe there's a lesson to be learned."

"Has there ever been a single damned company, a company which poisons our water, destroys our environment, that has ever been fined $50,000?" asked Louis Laberge. "But this Liberal judge didn't hesitate for a second to fine a union of 700-800 members $50,000. There has never been a goddam giant company fined as much in Quebec."

But the Liberals were preparing more to come. They were quietly drafting Bill 19.

On Wednesday, the same day the judge went into action, the Common Front met at the Château Frontenac for the first time with a committee of cabinet ministers to discuss the latest offer.

Aside from l'Allier and Castonguay, there were Finance Minister Garneau and Education Minister François Cloutier, who slept through most of the so-called emergency meeting. Hanging over the Front's head was the threat of back-to-work legislation. The Common Front attempted, at the very least, to salvage the $100 minimum. They offered to reduce substantially demands for the highest-paid workers. Not a chance. Finally Marcel Pepin asked the Finance Minister point blank if he was ready to accept the $100 minimum if the Common Front arranged other salaries so that the government wouldn't have to increase its total payments by much.

Advised by one of his counsellors, *Le Devoir* reported, not to answer the question, Garneau finaly admitted that the fundamental reason for the refusal of the minimum wage was that the government couldn't upset the industrial structure, the state of the labour market—supply and demand—and private enterprise.

There was nothing left to do, except for the government to unveil Bill 19. Premier Bourassa said the time had come to tell the Common Front "enough is enough," as he introduced the bill to the National Assembly.

Labour leaders had been expecting legislation for some kind of moratorium. Instead, they got a harsh, repressive piece of legislation which, in effect, destroyed the unions. Bill 19, while allowing a month for more negotiations, permitted the government to impose a settlement by simple decree. In addition, the unions would be deprived of all their fundamental rights for a two-year period. It went way beyond normal back-to-work legislation.

It also provided for fines of from $5,000 to $50,000 per day against unions and union officials who went against the law. The 210,000 employees could be fined $250 a day each if they didn't immediately return to work. Conceivably, it could work out to $200,000,000 a day or more.

The National Assembly debated the bill for 24 hours, nonstop, before finally passing it on Friday afternoon, April 21, the 11th day of the strike.

The severity of the bill shocked Front leaders. Initially, they announced they would recommend civil disobedience.

Louis Laberge was extraordinarily upset. He compared the law to the laws of Hitler and Mussolini, saying it was only one step away from declaring unions illegal. Almost one-half of the CNTU membership had lost their union rights as defined by law; a total of 210,000 workers were all but decertified.

"I know," said Laberge, "that there are many citizens who are happy that this special law has been adopted because our strike causes inconvenience and perhaps social malaise. But the citizens of Quebec should not rejoice. If the Bourassa government can do this to 210,000 who are exercising a recognized right, imagine what they can do to individuals.

"In the short term, citizens may feel comfortable, but that's exactly what happened in Germany and Italy when Hitler and Mussolini deprived citizens of their rights."

Even Labour Minister Jean Cournoyer was shaken by the legislation. It was apparent that the hardliners and not the so-called progressive faction of the cabinet had drafted the legislation. "They're crazy," said Cournoyer in a private conversation, "a thing like this could provoke serious disorders." After the passage of the law, the Common Front went into a huddle to decide on a course of action.

While the Common Front leaders spent Friday night debating a course of action, the right wing of the CNTU moved to scuttle resistance. The three right-wing members of the central's five-man executive—vice-president Paul-Emile Dalpé, treasurer Jacques Dion and director of services Amédée Daigle (known as "the three Ds")—called a snap meeting and voted to recommend respect for the law and a return to work.

This severely compromised the position of the two remaining members of the executive—president Marcel Pepin and general secretary Raymond Parent (known as "the two Ps"). The CNTU accounted for more than half the 210,000 strikers.

Voting results trickled into the Common Front's Quebec City headquarters at the Holiday Inn. About 65 per cent of the QFL and CNTU, and 53 per cent of the teachers voted to stay out. However, barely half the workers were able to participate in the hastily called vote. Once again, the most militant group was the poorly paid hospital workers.

Late Friday night the Common Front made up its mind. It recommended a return to work.

Union militants were shocked.

The three leaders needed most of the night to rally many of the militants to the decision, and were visibly pained by the strain of the situation. Le Devoir reported Marcel Pepin "had not yet recovered from the blow struck by his executive," Louis Laberge had traces of tears on his cheeks, and Yvon Charbonneau's white face was pinched with rage.

"One of the three must have worked for ITT," snapped one minor official on hearing the back-to-work order. There was some isolated sentiment among rank-and-filers to ignore the leaders' recommendation (in fact, some teachers and hospital maintenance workers stayed out a few more days).

The reasons for their decision, the three leaders explained, were the inconclusive results of the strike vote (the feeble turn-out may have been caused by resignation and apathy), and the fear that if resistance was mainly centred in the hospital sector, the workers could be severely bludgeoned on the picket lines.

Further, the statement by the three Ds seriously weakened the solidarity needed to defy Bill 19. Marcel Pepin, exhausted and torn by the CNTU executive split and without sleep for 60 hours, said it was against his will that he had made the back-to-work recommendation.

"I have changed a lot in two years," he told a reporter on the drive back to Montreal. "Now I believe it's better to accept the risk of violence than to capitulate on our demands for a new social order."

But that was not to be. The strikers were already moving back to work. The Quebec labour movement had apparently suffered a resounding defeat.

Quebec's conservative French and English papers were jubilant.

"The young government of Robert Bourassa was better prepared and more astute than the labour leadership," cheered the Montreal *Gazette*. "It was ironic to see the two more influential members of the labour leadership—Marcel Pepin and Laouis Laberge—negotiating with ministers 20 years their junior, and losing every round in the 10-day-long battle of wits."

In Montreal, the two regional labour outfits—the QFL's Montreal Labour Council and the CNTU's Central Council—held meetings over the weekend of April 22-23.

The QFL's Montreal group, previously a fairly conservative body which represented skilled workers—carpenters, plumbers, printers and the like—was holding a long-planned orientation congress. The mood of the delegates was apparent from discussions Saturday morning in the workshop on the economy. For instance, a vote was taken on a resolution advocating collective ownership of the means of production and workers' self-management. The ballot was 98 in favour and four against. Although few of the delegates represented workers from the public sector, Bill 19 was a main topic of angry discussion.

Over at the CNTU, Marcel Pepin attended the emergency meeting of the Central Council where he faced a deluge of bitterness over the decision to return to work. The Council accused the Front leaders of having missed the chance of a lifetime. Urged on by president Michel Chartrand, the Council called for a May 1 general strike by all organized labour. It also demanded the resignation of the three Ds.

Local union leaders from all Common Front affiliates agreed to consult their memberships, but some were doubtful such a massive action could be polled and organized on short notice.

Chartrand, who for years has been trying to get May 1 recognized as workers' day instead of the official September Labour Day, was adamant as he feverishly tried to get the general strike going.

But by Thursday it appeared to all concerned—except Chartrand—that the move was impossible.

By that day, April 27, QFL general secretary Fernand Daoust and Marcel Pepin—both initially sympathetic to the idea—declared it was "technically impossible to organize the strike," but that they were exploring other means of protest. Pepin's position within the CNTU was strengthened when the 24-man Confederal Bureau expressed unanimous approval of his leadership, and in effect censured the three Ds for publicly denouncing Pepin's words and conduct.

Union militants were organizing information meetings across the province. Inside union ranks, there was unanimous denunciation of Bill 19. The Bourassa government was condemned for giving in to the "fascist corporations and business community."

"St. James Street," declared one St-Jérôme worker, "wants to keep Quebec as a source of cheap labour. They won't let Bou-Bou give us a decent wage."

Although feeling was running high, the movement

couldn't pull together on a single means of expressing its anger.

On Thursday, the Quebec justice department moved, unwittingly, to give labour its chance. During the week, the Big Three—Pepin, Laberge and Charbonneau—had said local hospital workers shouldn't bear the sole responsibility of going to jail, since they had all urged them to disobey injunctions.

The three were summoned to appear in court on Thursday, May 4.

The right-wing media were pleased, saying jail sentences for the leaders would teach them to think twice before violating the law.

"We'll go to the court," Laberge said, "and I'll plead guilty with pride."

Throughout this time, the government was still expressing confidence that a negotiated settlement could be worked out.

But despite the government's public avowals of good will towards the unions and denials that it was out to crush the Front, many observers, including at least one cabinet minister, privately questioned the haste with which the Big Three were brought to court by the justice department.

"If the government really wants a peaceful settlement," said one civil servant, "I don't see why [justice minister] Choquette is pushing the Front. It seems like a provocation. After all, they can wait to press charges when the climate improves somewhat. They never did a damn thing to the Montreal and Provincial police when they went on illegal strikes. At least the Common Front was engaged in a legal operation."

He noted that when medical specialists had defied the government and stayed out on an illegal strike two years earlier, demanding an increase over the official offer of $52,000 a year, no charges had been laid; but hospital workers on strike for a minimum $100-a-week wage were getting six months in jail and $5,000 fines for a legal strike.

The Common Front leaders appeared briefly before the parliamentary committee on the public service and deposited their voluminous studies and demands. Pepin repeated his charge that the government wouldn't accede to the $100 minimum wage because they were unwilling to upset the capitalist labour market. Finance Minister Garneau, sitting off to his side, avoided Pepin's accusing eyes.

May 1 came and there was no strike.

In Montreal, several thousand people showed up at the Paul Sauvé arena to celebrate the founding of the Montreal regional front, composed of the Montreal Labour Council, the Central Council and the various teachers' groups. In a series of short speeches, the representatives pledged to work with all progressive groups, welfare recipients, unemployed and students, and to promote the local Comités d'Action Politique (CAPs) and generally lead the fight against capitalism, reaction and Bill 19.

Afterwards there was a beer and cider party, and dancing to the new revolutionary music popular in Quebec.

Labour was in a militant mood, but was still groping for a way to deal with the situation.

Three days later, the Quebec City judiciary bumbled into action.

In the morning, Superior Court Judge Pierre Coté sentenced 15 more union men to jail for violating injunctions. The leaders were due to be tried at 2 p.m.

The three men came up from Montreal and arrived shortly before the appointed hour, accompanied by a large contingent of supporters. Others were crammed into every nook and cranny of the small, oak-panelled courtroom. Actually, there wasn't much room for supporters. The court was filled with security guards and plainclothesmen, including a couple of Bourassa's personal bodyguards.

When the three marched into the courthouse, they couldn't get through the mob and into the courtroom. Somebody said there was a bigger courtroom down the hall, and everybody, led by Laberge, Pepin and Charbonneau, trooped in—security men, plainclothes detectives, supporters.

They sat and waited for the judge.

Before he arrived the riot squad, bedecked in leather and black visors and carrying long, black truncheons, muscled their way into the already crowded courtroom. Marcel Pepin noted the buildup of hardware and began to get angry. Still, there was no judge. Pepin consulted his watch, noted the time (2:30), looked at his two co-accused, and saw they understood what was happening.

"Let's go," he said, and the three leaders of Quebec's

unions got up and walked out of the courtroom. Through the marble halls of the courthouse they strode, followed by a frantic crowd of reporters and heralded by an advance guard of television cameramen grinding away.

"I'm not going to sit in there with the riot squad behind me," said Pepin.

"You saw them, the ton-ton matraques," Laberge said. "With their big sticks. It's like a banana republic. If they want to arrest us, they know where to find us. We're not in hiding."

The judge showed up 15 minutes later, called a brief recess, and then proceeded with the trial. He listened to government tapes of the union leaders and announced he would issue his verdict later.

Justice Minister Jérôme Choquette admitted that the presence of the riot squad in the courthouse had been "a mistake" but that the three men should not have walked out. Many unionists regarded the presence of the riot squad as another example of justice department provocation.

The verdict was announced Monday, May 8.

Marcel Pepin, Louis Laberge and Yvon Charbonneau, the heads of Quebec's three top labour organizations, were sentenced to one year in jail each.

In a lengthy, 28-page judgment (printed in full in most French papers), the judge quoted from U.S. Supreme Court decisions, John F. Kennedy, a British Columbia court ruling against the United Fishermen and Allied Workers, and several other sources to justify the maximum possible sentences.

"This sentence should take effect immediately," wrote the judge. "Any lesser sentence would leave the Judge feeling that, without reason, he failed the duty dictated by his conscience."

(The decision was actually a "collegial" one, made in consultation with other Superior Court justices.)

The severity of the one-year term stunned union members.

"That's justice, that's the democracy of the Liberal hacks," said one bitter teacher.

"That's the justice of the system," said Louis Laberge, "while big corporations are fined $75 or $500 for polluting our rivers, killing people or breaking the law, we—the criminals—must go to jail for exercising a right—the right to strike."

It was late Monday afternoon, but the groundswell of anger was already apparent.

At union meetings that night—a continuous custom in Quebec in the past few months—the members denounced the judiciary, government and business for collusion.

On Tuesday morning, the leaders and hundreds of sympathizers gathered outside the CNTU headquarters on St-Denis Street for the trip to Quebec City where they were to turn themselves in.

Even as the motorcade made its way along the South Shore highway to Quebec City, the walkouts and protests began. There had been no order given; from the first it appeared spontaneous. Around 11 a.m. longshoremen—never active in Common Front activities—walked off the job in Montreal, Trois-Rivières and Quebec City (only three weeks before, the 3,500 ILA members had signed a new contract).

By noon, 5,000 teachers in Joliette, the Gaspé, Chicoutimi, l'Estrie, Sorel, Mont-Laurier and the Mille Iles had joined the protest.

Canadian Union of Public Employees (CUPE) maintenance workers set up picket lines in several CEGEPs and a few hospitals. Groups of nurses and CNTU hospital workers joined them.

At 2 o'clock, the families of the three leaders joined three or four thousand workers at St-Louis Gate at the Quebec City Wall. The longshoremen showed up and volunteered to act as marshals. The throng started to march with Laberge, Pepin and Charbonneau to the courthouse.

The sun was shining as a grimy longshoreman approached to shake Pepin's hand. Pepin's 12-year-old daughter Marie was crying. Michel Pepin, eight, marched alongside his father. The longshoreman took Marcel Pepin's hand and said, "Don't worry, Marcel, we'll take care of your family while you're in jail."

The workers delivered the three to justice department officials, shouting solidarity and vowing they'd make the Quebec government know how they felt. The three were taken off to Orsainville prison on the outskirts of the city to begin their terms.

As the news was announced on the radio stations of the

province, right-wing commentators expressed satisfaction and declared that law and order had triumphed. They noted that there had been some protest, as expected, but nothing on a large scale.

That evening, in the remote North Shore town of Sept-Iles, several hundred miles down river from Quebec City, a few hundred workers gathered for a protest outside the local courthouse. Police tried to break it up, and a battle ensued. It was the spark that started the revolt.

The workers of Quebec were about to rise up by the thousands in one of the greatest displays of solidarity this country has seen since the Winnipeg general strike in 1919. The workers were to show hostility to a government dedicated to the interests of business. But above all, they were to show that the new militancy of the Quebec trade-union movement comes from the base, and is not dictated from the top. The revolt was the first, tentative step by the workers of Quebec to shrug off their old fears and to defend their class interest.

Late Tuesday and early Wednesday, the Sept-Iles workers had organized several meetings and voted massively to strike. Within a matter of hours, thousands of unionized workers brought the rich iron ore port to a standstill. The strike committee proceeded to take control of the town, and seized the radio station.

In St-Jérôme, a light industrial area with heavy unemployment 40 miles north of Montreal, the 400 employees of Regent Knitting Mills walked out. They were joined by the bus drivers, Secor metal plant workers, teachers and white-collar workers. At the invitation of unionized workers at CKJL radio station, the strike committee took over and started to broadcast revolutionary music and union statements.

The movement mushroomed across the province.

By Thursday 80,000 construction workers were off the job, along with workers at the Manicouagan 3 dam. Miners joined the protest in Thetford Mines, Asbestos and Black Lake. Workers shut down factories all across the province, including 23 at the St-Jérôme Industrial Park alone.

Mass meetings were held throughout the province.

In Sept-Iles one 52-year-old steelworker had tears in his eyes as he told a reporter: "They put Louis in jail. They can't do this. If we let them, they can put us all in jail, any one of us."

By Friday, radio announcers were left breathless as they read off lists of plants closed, walkouts, towns occupied, radio and television stations seized. For much of the Conservative and Liberal media, the situation seemed to be bordering on revolution. The shutdowns were blamed on a "small minority" of revolutionary agitators and goon squads.

Yet the majority of walkouts took place after mass meetings and votes. It took a lot of conviction to walk out since all the strikes (with the exception of Montreal's 8,000 blue-collar workers) were illegal and violated hard-won contracts. A typical case involved the Sir George Williams University library workers, where a majority walked out shortly after having won a long strike battle for union recognition from a management which had previously resisted all organizing attempts.

In many cases, work stoppages were the result of other strikers visiting work sites and asking—sometimes demanding—that their fellows join them in a demonstration of worker solidarity. On occasion, in the heat of the situation, there were incidents of heavy-handed "requests" brought on by inflamed passion.

But certainly, the massive, widespread response couldn't be attributed to "thugs and goon squads," as Robert Bourassa repeatedly claimed. Countless small plants, some with fewer than 25 employees, shut down and stayed shut for a day or a week.

In the Thetford Mines area, 8,000 workers downed tools within the space of two to three hours. All it took was one group to initiate the action. The rest moved spontaneously as word got around.

In Chibougamau the general shutdown was provoked by an angry group of women, some of them teachers and hospital workers. They marched to one of the mines and pulled their husbands off the job. It was only a matter of time before the effect was total.

A few groups, like the militant elementary school teachers who blocked bridges by dumping kegs of nails on the roadways, went slightly beyond peaceful protest. But on the whole, considering the scope of what was happening, there was remarkably little violence. One reason was that the actions were so widespread that police adopted a policy of non-intervention. Their power was too thinly spread. If they provoked a confrontation in one area, they wouldn't be able to contain the snowballing effect. For once, the police were too weak to provoke violence.

"The government thinks it can scare the workers by throwing their chiefs in jail," explained Michel Chartrand. "They think it's going to shut the workers up ... well, they set a forest fire which is going to spread everywhere, mobilizing thousands of workers in the private sector as well as the public sector."

Jean Labelle, a 28-year-old factory worker in St-Jérôme, offered a *New York Times* reporter a simple explanation: "What's our complaint? I guess the answer is that we're tired of being pushed around, and now, finally, we're pushing back. If we can show them, we're capable of anything."

Right-wing media commentators blamed the three Common Front leaders for the situation, saying that they should appeal their sentences and get out on bail. Yet the same commentators took NDP leader David Lewis to task for suggesting the sentences were due to the judge's "reckless ignorance," and answered that the sentences were fully justified. In almost the same breath, they were damning the leaders for going to jail and then supporting the harsh sentences.

The union position was that they'd rather serve their sentences right away than wait six months.

"It's no use to appeal," said Laberge, "because the system is rotten. And it's entirely rotten; it's not just rotten on one level."

A QFL statement said: "As far as we are concerned, we believe the police machine should push its logic to the extreme and lock everyone up who thinks like Laberge, Pepin and Charbonneau."

As the situation escalated, even some members of the business community wondered aloud if Bourassa had handled the conflict properly. "From an absolutely pragmatic point of view," delcared Charles Perrault, head of Le Conseil du Patronat, an employers' group, "history shows us that imprisoning union leaders rarely serves the cause of the state. It's a political conflict, and as much as this imprisonment is unfavourable to the state, it's a good tactic for the leaders."

The protests continued.

At QFL headquarters in Montreal, one top official said that many of the permanent staff "had underestimated the base, the rank and file." The union militancy was surprising not only the government and the employers, but the leadership. "Louis Laberge called from jail saying he was expecting protests but nothing on this scale."

During the week, the office building at the corner of St-Denis and Ste-Catherine Street East, where the QFL and several affiliated unions are located, was the scene of continuous activity. Union officials and members were tramping up and down the stairs (the elevator operators were off on strike) singing the *Marseillaise*. Down the road at the CNTU the preference seemed to be for the *Internationale*, but the feeling was the same, as union bulletins and news flowed in from across the province.

The work stoppages took on interesting and imaginative forms.

At the General Motors plant in Ste-Thérèse, which has had a troubled history of management problems, autoworkers asked a few dozen workers from St-Jérôme to set up picket lines at the plant during lunch hour. Normally, the autoworkers eat inside the plant at the cafeterias. This time, however, they went out to eat, and when they returned they refused to cross the St-Jérôme pickets and never went back to work. The 2,000 autoworkers were out, and at the same time managed to avoid legal responsibility.

Late Thursday night, Montreal newspaper workers at *La Presse* and *Le Devoir* decided to walk out. They were joined by supporters at the two other French-speaking papers, *Journal de Montréal* and *Montréal-Matin*. Together, they went over to the two English-language papers, the *Gazette* and the *Star* to request they stop publishing for a day. They proved unwilling, despite what *Star* editor Frank Walker described as the visitors' "polite" attitude. However, after considering the situation, the two English papers decided not to publish "in order to protect the safety of our employees." (Common Front members regarded their coverage of the general strike as "hysterical and violently anti-union.") Even employees of the union-backed weekly *Québec-Presse* walked out for a day.

Employees at the Albert Prevost Institute, a mental

hospital in north-end Montreal, locked out management personnel and ran the place by themselves, proclaiming "North America's first liberated hospital."

By the end of the week, strikes and workers' control extended to Sept-Iles, Baie-Comeau, Port-Cartier and Haute-Rive on the North Shore, Chibougmau in the North West, Murdochville in the Gaspé and Thetford Mines.

In addition to these towns, workers seized control of radio stations—and in a few cases, TV outlets—in at least a dozen other localities, including Amos, New Carlisle, Rouyn-Noranda, Joliette, Sherbrooke and a few in the Montreal area for varying amounts of time.

In the controlled towns, local Common Front committees decided which merchants would be allowed to remain open. Invariably, large food stores, like A & P, Steinberg's and Dominion, representing big money, were ordered closed in favour of co-ops or small, family-owned stores. The latter were ordered not to take advantage of the situation and a strict price-freeze was enforced.

By far the most spectacular aspect of the labour revolt was the vehemence and swiftness with which it spread through outwardly placid provincial areas. The reasons for this are as varied as the regions affected.

"It's probably the outlying areas that are going to provoke the real changes in Quebec," explained Pierre Mercille of the CNTU's Laurentian Central Council. "For years, the ideas came from Montreal, but the most radical actions came from outside the metropolis: Cabano, Mont-Laurier, and now the massive walkouts of Sept-Iles, St-Jérôme, Sorel. In Montreal, it's so big and anonymous, it's difficult to have co-ordinated action. But in the little towns, the workers understand fast, they know themselves and they act."

The two hardest-hit areas, the St-Jérôme-Laurentian region and the North Shore, differ drastically, yet both demonstrated the same frustration, impotence and rage. St-Jérôme suffers from high unemployment (up to 35 per cent in late 1970) and, with the exception of a few big, new plants, pays low wages, often $2 an hour or less. It has all the urban facilities a town its size could provide, with easy access to metropolitan Montreal, a half-hour drive south on the Laurentian Autoroute.

Sept-Iles, on the other hand, is a frontier town, young,

late-twentieth-century suburb in its architecture, separatist, well-paid (it has the highest average income in Canada), a union town. Sept-Iles is a town which knows it is exploited and is mad, but doesn't want to go too far.

The workers of Sept-Iles put themselves at the head of the May revolt with something that looked like what Trotsky called "dual power." They didn't consider it dual; they thought it was simply power. They thought they controlled the town, and for a day—Wednesday, May 10, 1972—they did.

Then the provincial police came in, and a strange feeling took hold of Sept-Iles, the feeling of two forces circling each other. Two animals wary of each other, rule by dual power: something had to give. In the Russia that Trotsky described, it was the bourgeoisie; in Sept-Iles, after five days, it was the workers.

"The future? said Clément Godbout of the Sept-Iles Steelworkers local during the strike. "I see it as all right, because the workers have decided to stop fighting just for more money and have decided to fight for a new society . . . What kind of new society? Well, I talk the way I do for a reason—I'm a socialist."

His kind of socialism would include the nationalization of resource industries like iron ore, but would also fit in with René Lévesque; when Lévesque came on television and said the government should avoid provoking but the union men should be prudent too, it seemed to go down all right with him.

A young machinist talked about the reasons for the Sept-Iles revolt that went beyond Bill 19 and the jailing of the union chiefs: "There's automation. Iron Ore is putting in a $30 million investment next year in new machinery, and in my section, it'll mean guys laid off . . . The companies, they have no heart, eh? Acquired rights—they'll try to take them away from you. All that counts for them is the buck. Look, here's the book we negotiate from: present contract—union demand—company offer—result. Here we're fighting to hang on to things we already had—little things, French as the language which rules in contract interpreting—we haven't even gotten into our demands for new things."

He was asked what he wants—to take over the plants, to do away with the boss? "I don't think we want that." What does he want? "Changement. Changement." He said the French word in English, and it was a beautiful word, beautiful but vast. By what agent? "Well, I think the Parti Québécois can do a lot."

Sept-Iles is PQ. But that is a background fact to what happened there, not a key. People spoke more against Coiteux, the Liberal wood merchant who beat separatist Sept-Iles twice, in 1966 and 1970, with votes from the still-alienated Gilles Vigneault fishermen further down the coast, than for the PQ. A few OUI badges from the 1970 PQ campaign were worn, but it was NOUS stickers from the Common Front and a fist-projecting-from-a-peace-sign symbol of Sept-Ilien design that prevailed.

Valmore Tremblay, who lost to Coiteux in 1970, was still a big man, a curlyheaded, plain-talking giant, in workers' councils. But he was thought of less as a PQ man than as a union man, a founder of the Fédération des Travailleurs Unis, Sept-Iles' permanent common front of men and women of all the unions and even the non-unionized. Dr. Bainville, the PQ doctor, and Maître Desrosiers, the PQ lawyer, were around, advising, getting the arrested unionists bail, yes indeed. But the feel was union. The war was class.

By the weekend of May 13, the protests all over the province hadn't faded and the Bourassa government was becoming frantic. It was clearly surprised by the extent of the protests. It had counted on the three leaders to appeal their jail terms. On Saturday, the premier dispatched Liberal lawyer Roger Thibadeau to Orsainville prison to plead with Marcel Pepin to appeal and get out of jail. The lawyer was an old friend of Pepin's and had brought him a gift—a book entitled L'Humanité en Marche. It was inscribed "de notre amitié, Roger Thibadeau." Pepin smiled and said, "Thanks for the souvenir."

Up until this time, the government had confined itself to declaring it still hoped for a negotiated settlement—along with declarations from Justice Minister Choquette to the effect that police had everything under control.

From their prison, the Big Three issued a defiant statement: "Within the current union conflict, there is an overriding social struggle. The Liberal establishment . . . has chosen the clubbing of the workers as its trademark. This government has no social policy, and we know it.

"This government, as an employer, cowers before its real 'boss,' the private sector, and we know it. This government chooses to imprison those who disturb the cosmetics masking the colonized, and we know it.

"The ordinary people understand quickly that this government won't, and cannot truly negotiate, because the men who belong to it are themselves held at the throat by the financiers or the men in Ottawa; and it is to them that they owe their power, not to the ordinary people.

"Repression turns a simple panic into a battle; a participant into a combatant; a diverse group of individuals into a force of solidarity . . . and finally, it obliges everyone to choose sides.

"Let us leave this government to its folly, to its judges and its useless, repressive laws, to its grey solitude in the image of a Brinks truck. The union and social cause for which we are fighting is just. We will win it by our resistance and our determination."

Meanwhile, a crowd of about 3,000 people gathered outside the prison for what was billed as "le Woodstock syndical." The park beside the prison assumed a festival atmosphere as a tent city was set up, complete with stands selling foods, homemade jams, T-shirts decorated with the Big Three in prison garb and crafts.

In between the music, people like Michel Chartrand, Marcel Perreault, Chartrand's counterpart at the QFL's Montreal Labour Council, and Robert Chagnon, of the Montreal Alliance des Professeurs, harangued the crowd. All three had been symbolically kidnapped the day before in Montreal, and delivered to the festival by militant teachers.

Chartrand took the opportunity to denounce René Lévesque and the attitude of the Parti Québécois. "These are the guys," he told the participants, "who want an institutionalized union movement, integrated into the capitalist system. We don't need bums like that to tell us what to do."

He had less kind things to say about Robert Bourassa who, at about that time, was hovering overhead in a helicopter, accompanied by Roads Minister Bernard Pinard—widely know as Mr. Patronage and one of the biggest dispensers of Liberal favours. After satisfying themselves that the Bolshevik mob wasn't about to run riot, the two ministers returned to the premier's new concrete bunker office-residence near the National Assembly.

Aside from the proletarian upheaval, Bourassa had to contend with an incipient palace revolt. The cabinet was severely shaken when it was learned that two of Bourassa's few able ministers—Social Affairs Minister Claude Castonguay and Public Service and Communications Minster Jean-Paul l'Allier—had tendered their resignations.

Although l'Allier, as public service minister, had been nominally responsible for negotiations with the Common Front and Castonguay's ministry was the biggest single employer, both men denied their dispute with the government had anything to do with the labour conflict.

They were angered by federal Finance Minister John Turner's spring budget. It had increased certain social services like old age pensions without consulting the province. For years, Quebec governments have had a running dispute with the federal government that centred on the demand to repatriate control of all social services, such as family allowances. Castonguay had been trying to create a coherent social security policy for the province, bringing all these monies and measures under provincial jurisdiction.

Both ministers felt the new budget violated federal-provincial understandings, and that the premier had been feeble in presenting Quebec's case. The crisis of confidence in Bourassa was so strong on this matter that Labour Minister Jean Cournoyer, himself indirectly involved in the labour crisis, had denounced his own government in a Parliamentary Commission two days before.

Visibly angry and pounding his fist on the table, he told Parti Québécois House Leader Camille Laurin: "You've made your choice, but I haven't made it as yet. But between you and me, I've had it up to here, my fists are ready ... If the government is capable of standing up to the union movements, they'd better stand up to the federal government."

Agriculture Minister Normand Toupin agreed with him.

Somehow, Premier Bourassa managed to cool the dissidents. Both Castonguay and l'Allier said they would withdraw their resignations, at least until the Liberals had weathered the labour storm.

Two days later, in another bid to get negotiations going with the Common Front, Bourassa took the public service portfolio away from l'Allier and gave it to Cournoyer. L'Allier retained the communications portfolio.

Quebec labour leaders have never been hostile to Cournoyer; in fact, many even like him. The same can be said, to a lesser degree, about l'Allier. But it can't be said for the rest of the cabinet which decides policy, so it's difficult to understand what Bourassa hoped to accomplish with this supposed conciliatory move.

The union protest and revolt was now in its eighth day. Aside from this minor portfolio switch, the government had done little except wait it out and hope public opinion, whipped up by the media, would force the Front into capitulation.

The Liberals, in fact, decided the media, already bordering on hysteria, weren't enough. And so the party embarked on one of the more bizarre escapades of the conflict in an attempt to break the unions.

Early in the week, a staffer of the Teachers Corporation intercepted a secret telex message to the Liberal Party's 108 riding presidents. The message, sent by party president Lise Bacon, ordered local Liberal associations to set up, in effect, vigilante committees.

They were told to "gather information on local disturbances, arouse public opinion against the strikers and find ways of ensuring order themselves." One of the ways suggested was to pressure local authorities to swear in party stalwarts and toughs as "special constables." In two towns at least, Baie-Comeau and Haute-Rive, a total of over 200 civilians were sworn in.

Meanwhile, Justice Minister Choquette, the government's most persistent hardliner, assured the populace that the police had "complete control over the situation" and that there was "no reason, for the moment," to take additional measures. He said police power was concentrated in 14 strategic points in the province and ready to move in if necessary.

On Tuesday, May 15, 34 local union officials decided to renounce their bail and join the Big Three at Orsainville prison.

Another huge crowd turned out in Quebec City for the latest surrender of prisoners, representing "le monde ordinaire." The scene was even more emotional and bitter than the surrender ceremonies the week previous.

"One thing I can never forget," said 51-year-old Mme Louise Leblanc, a hospital worker from Notre Dame de Lourdes in Montreal, "is that I have been condemned for having defended the cause of the workers." She was accompanied by her daughter who, like herself, was sentenced to six months in prison and a personal fine of $5,000, but who had elected to stay out and care for the family.

The group marched from the Cross of Sacrifice monument to the courthouse, carrying the Front's latest poster bearing a photo of hospital worker Doris MacDonald. It stated simply: "I was a peaceful woman, but today I have anger in my heart."

"Tell Mr. Richard, the personnel director at St-Jean de Dieu Hospital, that his prisoners have a message for him," muttered another worker. "Tell him we're not giving up, we're going to spend our time in jail reading about the labour movement and politics and we're going to come out stronger than ever."

While some strikers were returning to work, they were being replaced by others, such as the Liquor Board employees, 1,500 shop workers at the Canadair plant and 650 National Harbours Board office workers. Another 135 schools were reported closed in the Eastern Townships, the Trois-Rivières region and Quebec City suburbs, while some 700 Hydro-Québec workers joined the protest.

But the Liberal Party's offensive against the unions was gathering steam. An anti-strike meeting of construction workers was organized at the Jean Béliveau arena on Montreal's South Shore. Although it purported to be a union meeting, it was later revealed that rental costs for the arena were picked up by the Montreal Association of General Contractors. The contractors had given non-union personnel and unionized workers who had refused to strike the day off, to attend the meeting and later disrupt an official union meeting. At the second meeting, the two groups clashed outside the Paul Sauvé arena. Police separated the two camps and then provided the anti-strike faction with megaphones and loudspeakers to harangue the strikers.

The leading speakers were small-time contractors, many of whom depend on the good graces of the party in power to stay in business. At least two of the anti-strike meeting leaders were identified as Liberal organizers.

The same day that the 34 new prisoners turned themselves in, the new public service minister, Jean Cournoyer, got in touch with the jailed Front leaders and said he was now prepared to negotiate a "true settlement." The three were inclined to accept Cournoyer's good faith. He was regarded as an honest labour minister and seemed genuinely interested in negotiating a collective agreement outside the framework of Bill 19.

Wednesday afternoon, QFL general secretary Fernand Daoust, speaking for the Front, announced a truce and called for an end to all work stoppages. The government, he said, was prepared to talk. It was understood that the Big Three would be released on probation, as provided by law.

By Thursday, Quebec's labour revolt had ground to a halt and the workers streamed back to their jobs. The Front had reason to believe that Cournoyer was empowered to enact a conciliatory agreement. Cournoyer also believed this.

However, the cabinet was divided and Justice Minister Choquette moved to undermine Cournoyer's position and stamp out all efforts at conciliation. Choquette, who has moved to consolidate his power over Quebec's police forces and increase his influence in the Liberal Party apparatus since the October FLQ Crisis, had decided that an immediate release of the union men would be interpreted as a sign of weakness.

Despite the fact the union had lived up to its part of the bargain and despite Cournoyer's attempts to obtain their release—abetted, it is believed, by both Castonguay and l'Allier—the three remained in jail.

As the government tried to outmanoeuvre the Front, the Liberal Party engaged in promoting the destruction of union solidarity. Their tools were to be the ambitious three Ds, Dalpé, Dion and Daigle, the right-wingers in the CNTU executive.

The three Ds accused Pepin of "odiously misrepresenting" the membership, saying, in the words of Dalpé, he "preferred, to the detriment of negotiations, the easy oasis of prison . . . and, as everyone knows, at the expense of the taxpayers." The three then went about the task of attempting to wreck union solidarity better than any employer or government.

They organized an ad hoc meeting of about 1,000 dissident union officials in Quebec City to decide whether to "clean out the CNTU of leftist and revolutionaries," or else to break up the CNTU and start their own "non-political" union central. They opted for the latter.

Their actions shocked CNTU loyalists, normally a thick-skinned, rough-hewn breed.

Actually, the "mutinous treachery," as the left-wingers called it, was the culmination of the long battle within the union central over politicization. The battle was building up for a showdown at the annual convention scheduled for June 11. It became increasingly apparent to the right-wingers, mostly relics of the old Catholic Confederation days, that they were in for a resounding defeat over the adoption of the *Ne comptons que sur nos propres moyens* manifesto.

Raymond Parent, the secretary-general loyal to Marcel Pepin, was convinced that the mini-revolt was organized by the Liberals. Within the CNTU, a number of union officials still adhere to the Liberal Party, some of them working as party organizers. One of the men lurking in the background behind the three Ds was Jacques Olivier, a former treasurer of the CNTU's Fédération Nationale des Services and a hospital union official. In May 1972 he was working for the Prime Minister's Office in Ottawa.

At any rate, the three Ds were unable to muster enough support, as the vast majority of union leaders and members rallied to uphold their imprisoned president and preserve the CNTU's integrity and direction.

Three of the CNTU's eleven federations, which group members according to sector—Wood and Construction, Clothing, and Textiles—voted to support the three Ds. But within these federations—for example construction workers in Sept-Iles, St-Jérôme and other regions—large groups decided to pull out and stay in ranks.

Naturally, the internal conflict, brought full-blown into the public view, caused nothing but glee within Liberal ranks especially as it came while the Front was still seeking the release of the Big Three.

Cabinet Minister Cournoyer was trying desperately, as he had promised, to obtain their release on day parole.

However, the hardliners, led by Justice Minister Choquette, sabotaged all attempts. The latter claimed it was simply an administrative decision, left to judicial authorities without political interference. In fact, the decision not to release the three was decided finally at a Liberal Party caucus meeting.

Urged on by Cournoyer, who promised he would obtain a negotiated settlement of the public service conflict and make amendments to Bill 19 (and prompted by the three Ds' mutiny), Pepin, Laberge and Charbonneau finally opted to appeal their sentences. Along with the other imprisoned unionists, they were released on Tuesday, May 23.

Once out, Pepin called a meeting of the CNTU's ruling Confederal Council which voted by a 117 to 7 margin to expel the three Ds. (The three had refused to resign although they were openly working against the union.)

The dissidents refused to participate in the CNTU convention (it is recognized even by hostile critics that the CNTU has possibly the most democratic structure of any union outfit in North America). Instead, the three Ds held their own ad hoc convention one week before. The hastily convoked conclave formed a new union central called La Centrale des Syndicats Démocratiques—the Central of Democratic Trade Unions.

The CSD immediately claimed a potential membership of 45,000, while the press gleefully predicted that probably 80,000 workers would vote to disaffiliate from the CNTU. In the next few weeks, literally hundreds of unions were called out to pronounce themselves for or against the CNTU. Three months later, the CSD legally claimed to represent slightly under 19,000 Quebec workers.

However, the Liberal government quickly amended certain bits of labour legislation—such as the law concerning the construction industry which names the CNTU and QFL as the only legal bargaining agents—to legitimize the CSD's position, thus encouraging future raiding.

Despite the irritation caused by the right-wingers, morale within the CNTU was very high, especially amongst the people who felt the conservatives had slowed the movement's evolution in the past.

"When I got out of jail," said Pepin, "I sensed an impression of incredible vitality in the ranks ... one inning of the game is over, the dynamic forces of syndicalism have grouped together . . . Our action necessarily causes upheavals as we really try to ensure that political and economic decisions are no longer made by a powerful minority."

The cumulative effects of the April-May events have resulted in an even greater radicalization and politicization of Quebec workers than was believed possible. The Common Front was solidified by joint action at the local and regional level in countless cases.

Louis Laberge said when he got out of jail: "Yes, I've changed since October 29 [date of the violent *La Presse* demonstration]. If you want, they talk of my radicalization, that's OK with me. I'm no longer the same guy that I was. Because I used to believe in the damn system. I don't believe in it anymore. If we continue to accept St. James Street, we'll never get out of the hole."

What happened to Louis Laberge has now happened to thousands upon thousands of Quebec workers.

The crisis revealed the deep currents of politicization of certain sections of the working class, and speeded up a similar trend in other areas. It showed the hollowness of traditional liberalism, and increased a polarization of class sentiment. In so doing, the workers of Quebec may have laid the foundations of an opposition dedicated to furthering workers' interests.

The government beat back the revolt, and may well try to stifle the movement permanently through more repressive legislation. Through the Liberal Party and its supporters, attempts are being made to erode and divide the union movement.

But the movement has shown it has a solid base. "The government of Monsieur Bourassa is only a step away from pushing unionized workers into resistance and clandestinity," declared Louis Laberge. "He has only to declare the union movement illegal. But he shouldn't rub his hands so quickly. We haven't decided to let ourselves be beaten."

The drive towards a new society in Quebec has started in earnest. Most of the labour movement is committed to it. There is a new enthusiasm that becomes apparent in discussions with union officials and the rank-and-file militants.

There is a desire to do away with a bureaucratic unionism that fits neatly into its place in the system, and to return to the roots of trade unionism. There is a desire to get away from seeking a little more an hour for the labour elite, and to fight for the interests of all workers, unionized and non-unionized.

"Not since the days of the Industrial Workers of the World, since the days of Joe Hill and the battle for the eight-hour day," says Marcel Pepin, "has a North American union movement been so dedicated to the tradition of revolutionary syndicalism."

Afterword

In the fall of 1971, the left in Quebec was groping for a new path. "I'm beginning to have my fill of nationalism," one young radical said. "I've been fighting for socialist independence for years, but now I feel like moving to Saskatchewan. The English are quieter, but at least they have a socialist movement."

The only steady current that could be perceived was the Parti Québécois. Although many leftists worked for it, none was satisfied with it, and its growing acceptance of the existing social system posed a problem for the left and the increasingly radical trade-union movement. It was in this context that the Vallières-Gagnon debate erupted.

Charles Gagnon gave an interview in September to a reporter from the Montreal *Gazette* who had co-authored an openly right-wing account of the War Measures Act crisis, and said that the FLQ had outlived its usefulness and what was needed now was a mass-based, aboveground workers' party.

Around the same time, Gagnon's long-time comrade-in-arms Pierre Vallières, only recently released from jail, jumped bail and dramatically went underground.

Vallières's action seemed to indicate a split with his old colleague, and it did—but the split was not as it at first appeared. For if Vallières gave the impression of clinging to the romantic, flamboyant revolutionism of the late sixties, that impression did not last long. In December he wrote a long letter to *Le Devoir* in which he agreed with Gagnon's negative position on terrorism and the FLQ, but went even further and opted to support the PQ.

"Che Guevara stresses," wrote Vallières, "that it should never be excluded *a priori* that a revolutionary change in a given society can be started by an electoral process. All the better, it should be added, if this change can be achieved totally by this process ... In the present situation it would be an unpardonable error for the partisans of a real social revolution in Quebec to underestimate or, worse, to deny what the Quebec people can gain by the strategy which has been defined by the Parti Québécois."

While underground he and other members of the FLQ had undergone an "autocritique"—an examination of their political position. After the autocritique was over the group had reached unanimity on the question of armed agitation but not on the PQ. There was the same division in the Quebec left as a whole. While many agreed with Vallières, others denounced him vehemently—among them Charles Gagnon. The intense debate that was going on was thrown into sharp focus by the new positions of the two former Felquistes.

To a degree, the debate had already been overtaken by events. By the time Vallières finished his autocritique, the *La Presse* demonstration had introduced a new era in the Quebec labour movement, *Ne comptons que sur nos propres moyens* had appeared, and thousands of workers at both the November 2 Montreal Forum rally and the QFL convention had cheered Louis Laberge as he called for the overthrow of the regime. Events were moving so quickly that it didn't seem the time for arguments over strategy.

But in another sense, the fast-changing orientation of the trade unions gave the debate a new urgency. For the labour movement and the new left-wing coalition still lack a political vehicle. The Parti Québécois, whose chief denounces "the ranting and raving of labour leaders," seems unwilling to be that vehicle. And to set up a separate workers' party may be to split the opposition and ensure the continued success of the Liberals.

It is not an easy dilemma to resolve, but it will have to be resolved if the labour movement seriously intends to pursue its social and political goals. The developments that began to take place in the Quebec labour movement in 1971 are remarkable, but they are not without precedent in this country. They occurred in Winnipeg in 1919. Even in supposedly tranquil Nova Scotia, severe sentences handed out to striking fishermen for defying injunctions in 1970 touched off a series of spontaneous walkouts in various parts of the province; unlike their Quebec counterparts two years later, the Nova Scotian workers succeeded in forcing the release of the jailed trade unionists.

The left in Quebec has developed rapidly, and is still developing rapidly. If it can now develop in the direction of a political organization, it may go off on the "road to glory" that even Liberal organizers have marked out for it.

Postscript

In the difficult times surrounding the birth of trade unionism, is was relatively easy to identify the oppressor. The simple identification of the master and the slave was clear to the naked eye. The boss was known, he was greedy, and if he did not crack the whip himself, we knew he was controlling the arm which was. The labour movement then retaliated using the only available and essential weapons: courage, solidarity and determination in battle. Today, one may easily be lulled to sleep by the anonymity of the oppressors, their replacement by a seemingly objective bureaucratic apparatus. One in the end may even believe that multi-national corporations have many cats to skin besides the workers and that the time of sadistic bosses is past.

But have things changed so deeply? Isn't our society still motivated by the maximization of profit? Do not the beneficiaries of such maximized profits still represent a small minority of a privileged few? Are not those privileged few still strongly protected by the political and the judiciary? Are not the workers still at the mercy of an economic system which governs their social and political life? Are they not still prevented from exercising any control over the orientation and development of those empires which are crushing them?

We believe that in Quebec over the past two years, we have been given a rather clear answer to all those questions. We, the wage earners, were violently reminded of our state of dependence. We were told in no uncertain terms what interests the political powers in Quebec and Ottawa want to serve. And even more cynically, we were made to understand our true weight and the precise place we held as a community, as Quebec workers, in the evolution of what we still call "our" society.

The cards are on the table. Empires like Power Corporation are not hiding anything anymore. They coldly tell us that to satisfy the requirements for maximum profitability, they must unload more than half the human tools they have been using for 25 to 30 years. They tell us they must carry out this operation freely, with flexibility, and that the organizations that the workers have been able to forge through great effort over 100 years are obstacles to the rationalization of their operations. And those obstacles are then removed. This was what Power Corporation was deliberately trying at *La Presse*, where it spent a fortune to break the back of the unions. This is what we call a clear-cut situation.

The turmoil of immediacy, if it did not give us much opportunity for rest, at least simplified the task of separating our allies from our enemies. We know the sides people are taking. We know for instance that on the one hand, the politicians and the judiciary are blessing the employers who, through their negligence and their greed for profit, assassinate workers on building sites, in mines, and in plants. We know that on the other hand, the same authorities do not hesitate one moment in setting up a military-police machine at an exorbitant cost as soon as they feel they may have any reason to believe that an apprehended insurrection may threaten the safety of a few well-off individuals. This is what we call a clear-cut situation.

Let us read just a few lines from a theorist of the colonial world: "In capitalist countries, between the exploited and the powerful there intervene a multitude of teachers of ethics, advisers, disorienters. In colonial areas, on the other hand, the policemen and the soldiers, through their immediate interventions, are directly in contact with the colonized and, with the butts of their rifles, advise them to stay in line. We can see that such an intermediary of the powerful uses a language of pure violence. He alleges no oppression, and does not disguise his domination. He exposes them, shows them with the good conscience of the forces of law and order. He takes violence right to the houses and minds of the colonized."

Do not those few words of Frantz Fanon, author of *Wretched Of The Earth*, have, since October 29, 1971, a very acute relevance for the workers in Quebec?

Until then, chambers of commerce, politicians, the clergy and even maybe, let's admit it, the labour movement, had succeeded in playing the role of the teachers of ethics that Frantz Fanon talks about. They had more or less convinced Quebecers that they were living in a capitalist society and consequently benefitted from its most profound values. But the direct intervention of brutal force as soon as the interests of a minute minority were at stake, leaves us in no doubt. Quebec has only accidentally participated in the capitalist paradise. As for the rest, its progress and weak and dependent political structures exactly correspond to the colonial model.

It is now clear that the old burden of human and material waste engendered by profit machines must be borne by the labouring class. On the other hand, the increase of capital, the economic expansion of large enterprises, the maximization of their profits, all these elements essential to the running of our good liberal economy, do not have as an automatic consequence the improvement of the standard of living of the worker. Quite the contrary, they tend to make him poorer.

It is important to keep all this in mind. We must get out of our mind those lulling economic principles we have been taught. We must stop believing those politicians and financiers who still sing the tune: "When the economy is buoyant, everything is fine" and "Industrial prosperity will promote social justice." We have received enough slaps in the face to stop believing that we have only to put gas in the economic machine for it to shower the people with heavenly goods. We have sacrificed enough generations of heads of families to understand that this machine does not primarily benefit us, the workers. Men are used as fuel: when they are burned out, they are rejected. Profits are accumulated in an increasingly small number of increasingly large pockets.

Traditional political authorities usually watch all this as silent accomplices. At least they did until recently. They were happy being merely the watchdogs of holy free enterprise. But then this passive role was not sufficient any more. They were no longer happy being merely spectators. Now they contribute impudently to the enrichment of those who fill their slush funds. They are not happy just to avoid counteracting the capitalist regime. They feed it. And this to such an extent that certain economists who are far from being revolutionary are worried when they see governments perverting the operation of the system by reducing to an insignificant proportion the risk for industrial and financial holdings overfed by subsidies. Conclusion: workers not only have to bear the burden imposed by the economic regime by suffering, for instance, rates of unemployment in excess of ten per cent and supporting a growing army of social welfare recipients, but in addition they have to dig into their pockets to pay for the gifts made to enterprises which are still not accountable, either to the government or the workers.

Subsidies are thrown about right and left, both by the federal government and by that of Quebec. In both cases, the game is played according to the rules of the economically powerful: 1. no true priority for economic and social developments; 2. no control on management, methods and nature of production, orientation or long-term intentions of the enterprise; 3. especially no participation of any kind in the profits.

The federal government started the waltz of subsidies. Its Quebec branch followed suit with alacrity. It is through such actions that we realize that these two political animals are of one flesh. We should not be deluded by superficial differences. Just because Trudeau announced that he was deliberately going to create unemployment while Bourassa was promising 100,000 jobs does not mean that we should believe that there is a deep difference. What is the difference, really, between the electoral promises of a varlet and the cynical actions of a petty king enjoying totalitarian powers?

The main consequence of such action by the government was to give a free hand to oppression. Not satisfied with emptying our pockets to provide direct or indirect subsidies to those profit machines, the large companies, the government lets them treat human material at their whim.

In Quebec as elsewhere in the American paradise, exploitation of the working class did not stop with the modernization of industry. Like the industry, the exploitation was modernized! And at the same time it became more rigorous. Capital is concentrated in a limited number of hands, and those hands are well armed to crush us better. They push us to work, where rhythms, standards and ratings must consistently be surpassed; productivity must always be increased and production costs reduced; when exhausted by industrial fatigue or sidelined by an accident, we are thrown in the gutter, the machines keep on; and the lines of unemployed welcomed by the industrialists and cynically created with the assistance of politicians of the Trudeau type desperately wait to take our places in the same inferno.

With the development of large industry and the apparent advance toward a certain economic stability, we had visions. We imagined that whole strata of more skilled wage-earners, better paid, with better job security, were being created, in a different class from other workers. We called them the middle class. We were fooled. We were lumping those workers we were told were privileged with the true privileged ones. We were telling ourselves, this guy has a house, two cars, colour TV; he takes his vacation in the South, he's like a boss. And many of those workers had actually acquired a bourgeois attitude which made them look like bourgeois rather than wage-earners. But it was only surface. We now find out how fragile their situation was. Several thousands of Quebec workers had a rude awakening in the last few years. The fellows in Canadair, who knew they were in one of the leading industries with the brightest prospects for expansion, began to see thousands of their brothers struck by a cynical drop in their economic condition. In other sectors that no one ever dreamed of as threatened, like pulp and paper, metallurgy, mines and chemical products, skilled workers are falling like flies. The strongest collective agreements gained courageously through long years of struggle and sacrifice are powerless to prevent the slaughter when, for reasons of increased profitability, investment priorities or plant modernizing, those who control and benefit from the economy decide to scrap, along with the old machines, men and women who do not quite fit in with the new plan.

Just a plant closure, an important technological change or the saturation of this or that skill on the labour market, is enough for a large percentage of the middle class to disappear. Gone with the wind. Those workers had forgotten that they were not members of the restricted group of true beneficiaries of the economic system. It was only accidentally, because of favourable conditions in the labour market and the economic situation, that they could be allowed to pose as well-off people for a limited time. Of course, this limited time could mean a whole lifetime. But not necessarily; that is, it is not owed them, the way profits are due the investor. The investor can have set-backs, but he will know that it was through bad administration or the dishonesty of a compètitor, if he did not get his expected return on investment. The man who invests his labour is a loser before he starts. He knows that his privilege of working may be withdrawn at any time. It exists totally independent of his will.

We must recognize each other. We are all united through our own dependence. A temporary and perishable surface coating alone makes us different one from another. In the past, efforts made to divide us by making some believe they were participating in the total happiness of the affluent society, sometimes convinced us. We said: "Let us not destroy this economic system; let us instead try to have everyone enjoy the same benefits."

Today, after being served the slap in the face of plant and mine closures, aggression of the *La Presse* type, increasingly frequent attempts to declassify skilled personnel, we cannot but revert to our original position. To raise the underprivileged workers to the level of those workers we considered privileged does not mean much anymore. Wage earners are all strangely similar. In the long run, we are all victims of the same economic activity. And only partially and provisionally, can a restricted number of us ever benefit.

Louis Laberge,
President of QFL

Marcel Pepin,
President of CNTU

Yvon Charbonneau,
President of Quebec Teachers Corporation

Appendix 1
Major Names in the Text

Archambault, Germain   Until his death in 1969, Montreal's chief taxi militant and strategist. Founder of the Mouvement de Libération du Taxi (MLT).

Bertrand, Jean-Jacques   Union Nationale premier of Quebec, 1968-1970. Before that justice and education minister in the cabinet of Daniel Johnson.

Bourassa, Robert   Economist, Liberal member of the National Assembly and after May 1970 premier of Quebec. Related by marriage to the powerful Simard shipbuilding family.

Bourgault, Pierre   Longtime head of the Rassemblement pour l'Indépendance Nationale (RIN), Quebec's first major separatist party. After 1968 a leading member of the Parti Québécois.

Castonguay, Claude   Author of the massive Castonguay report on social welfare in Quebec and after May 1970 minister of social affairs in the cabinet of Robert Bourassa. A leader of the liberal wing of the cabinet.

Charbonneau, Yvon   After 1970, president of the Quebec Teachers Corporation and one of the leaders of the Common Front of labour.

Chartrand, Michel   Wartime activist in the Bloc Populaire, militant at the Asbestos strike in 1949 and the Murdochville strike in 1957, leading member of the Parti Socialiste du Québec (PSQ) in the early sixties, and after 1968 president of the Montreal Central Council of the Confederation of National Trade Unions (CNTU) and leader of the left wing of the Quebec labour movement.

Choquette, Jérôme   After May 1970, justice minister in the cabinet of Robert Bourassa and the cabinet's leading hardliner.

Cournoyer, Jean   Union Nationale labour minister, 1969-1970, and after the assassination of Pierre Laporte, in October 1970, Liberal labour minister. A member of the liberal wing of the cabinet.

Desmarais, Paul After 1968, president of Power Corporation, the conglomerate with vast media, transport and other holdings in Quebec.

Diterlizzi, Frank Italian-born leader of "les gars de Lapalme," the out-of-work mail-truck drivers whose struggle became a symbol in Quebec after 1970.

Drapeau, Jean Unsuccessful anti-conscription candidate for the House of Commons in Outremont, 1942, anti-corruption crusader in Montreal in the early fifties, and mayor of Montreal from 1954 to 1957 and again after 1960.

Duplessis, Maurice Union Nationale premier of Quebec, 1936-1939 and 1944-1959. Nicknamed "le Chef" and known for his corrupt and dictatorial methods of government.

Ferretti, Andrée A leader of the Mouvement de Libération Populaire (MLP), 1964-1965, the left wing of the Rassemblement pour l'Indépendance Nationale (RIN), 1965-1967, and the Front de Libération Populaire (FLP), 1968-1969. Now works for the Confederation of National Trade Unions (CNTU).

Gagnon, Charles Along with Pierre Vallières, an ideological leader of the 1966 Front de Libération du Québec (FLQ), which was responsible for several bombings of strike-bound factories. Spent 1966 to 1970 in jail as a result of his FLQ activities; released early in 1970, arrested again under the War Measures Act in October and finally acquitted of all charges. Broke with the FLQ in September 1971.

Johnson, Daniel Union Nationale cabinet minister, 1958-1960, leader of the Union Nationale, 1961-1968, and premier of Quebec, 1966-1968. Author of *Equality or Independence*. Died in office September 1968.

Kierans, Eric President of the Montreal Stock Exchange, 1960-1963, minister of revenue and later minister of health in the cabinet of Jean Lesage, 1963-1966, president of the Quebec Liberal Party and the man responsible for forcing René Lévesque's resignation from the party, 1967, candidate for the federal Liberal leadership, 1968, and federal cabinet minister, 1968-1971.

Laberge, Louis After 1964, president of the Quebec Federation of Labour; a "moderate" in the sixties but in the early seventies a leader of the Common Front and of the new militancy in Quebec labour.

Laporte, Pierre Crusading journalist for *Le Devoir* in the late fifties, author of *The True Face of Duplessis*, minister of municipal affairs and cultural affairs in the cabinet of Jean Lesage, 1961-1966, candidate for the Quebec Liberal leadership, 1970, labour minister in the cabinet of Robert Bourassa, May-October 1970, killed by the Front de Libération du Québec (FLQ), October 1970.

Lemieux, Raymond Leader of the Mouvement pour l'Intégration Scolaire (MIS; later the LIS—Ligue pour l'Intégration Scolaire), a group demanding that French be the language of all schools in Quebec.

Lemieux, Robert Radical lawyer, defended many members of the Front de Libération du Québec (FLQ), including Pierre Vallières and Charles Gagnon; spokesman for the FLQ during the October 1970 Crisis.

Lesage, Jean Federal minister of northern development and natural resources in the cabinet of Louis St-Laurent in the fifties; provincial Liberal leader, 1958-1969, and premier of Quebec, 1960-1966. Presided over the Quiet Revolution.

Lévesque, René Radical journalist and broadcaster in the fifties; a leader of the Radio-Canada producers' strike, 1959; minister in the cabinet of Jean Lesage and leader of the left wing of the cabinet, 1960-1966; responsible for the nationalization of Quebec hydroelectric power companies, 1962; resigned from the Liberal Party in 1967 and formed the separatist Mouvement Souveraineté-Association (MSA), after 1968 the Parti Québécois (PQ). Author of *An Option for Quebec*, 1968.

Marchand, Jean Head of the Canadian Catholic Confederation of Labour (CCCL) and its successor, the Confederation of National Trade Unions (CNTU), until 1965. Along with Pierre Elliott Trudeau and Gérard Pelletier, one of the "three wise men" elected as Liberal members of the federal House of Commons in 1965. Federal minister of manpower and immigration, 1965-1968, and of regional economic expansion, after 1968. "Quebec lieutenant" to prime ministers Pearson and Trudeau.

Pelletier, Gérard In the fifties, radical journalist and trade-union activist and along with Pierre Elliott Trudeau a leading member of the left-liberal *Cité Libre* group. Editor-in-chief of *La Presse* in the early sixties. Along with Trudeau and Jean Marchand, one of the "three wise men" elected as Liberal members of the federal House of Commons in 1965.

Federal secretary of state after 1968. Author of *The October Crisis*, 1970.

Pepin, Marcel   President of the Confederation of National Trade Unions (CNTU) after 1965, and in the early seventies one of the leaders of the Common Front of labour.

Ryan, Claude   Editor of *Le Devoir* after 1964 and a leading Catholic nationalist. Accused of being a member of the spurious "provisional government" plot, 1970.

Trudeau, Pierre Elliott   In the fifties, radical journalist and political theorist and later professor of law at the University of Montreal. Along with Gérard Pelletier, a leading member of the left-liberal *Cité Libre* group. Along with Pelletier and Jean Marchand, one of the "three wise men" elected as Liberal members of the House of Commons in 1965. Federal minister of justice, 1967-1968, and prime minister after 1968. Invoked the War Measures Act, 1970. Editor of and author of the chief essay in *The Asbestos Strike*, 1956; author of *Federalism and the French Canadians*, 1968.

Vallières, Pierre   Successor to Pierre Elliott Trudeau as editor of *Cité Libre*, 1963; forced out, 1964. Along with Charles Gagnon, an ideological leader of the 1966 Front de Libération du Québec (FLQ), which was responsible for several bombings of strikebound factories. Spent 1966 to 1970 in jail as a result of his FLQ activities; released early in 1970, arrested again under the War Measures Act in October and released again in 1971. Broke with the FLQ in December 1971 and joined the Parti Québécois (PQ). Author of *White Niggers of America*, 1967, and *Choose!*, 1971.

Wagner, Claude   Law-and-order judge in the early sixties; justice minister in the cabinet of Jean Lesage, 1964-1966; unsuccessful candidate for the Quebec Liberal leadership, 1970; reappointed a judge, 1970; mentioned prominently as possible leader of Union Nationale and Créditiste parties, 1970-1971; leader of the Quebec wing of the federal Progressive Conservative Party, 1972.

Appendix 2
Major Organizations in the Text

Bloc Populaire Canadien Organization formed during World War II around the conscription issue and the leading voice of French Canadian nationalism at the time. Dissolved after the War.

CAP Comité d'Action Politique. One of a number of citizens' committees in various Montreal neighbourhoods organizing around local issues. The CAPs are grouped in the Front d'Action Politique (FRAP), the main opposition party to Mayor Jean Drapeau.

CCCL See CNTU.

CEQ Corporation des Enseignants du Québec (Quebec Teachers Corporation), the union of the 70,000 teachers employed in Quebec's French Catholic school system. One of the components of the Common Front.

CFIA Canadian Federation of Independent Associations, a federation of company unions often used by employers to keep real unions out.

Cité Libre Left-liberal journal of the 1950s and early 1960s around which were grouped some of the major figures in the coalition opposing Premier Maurice Duplessis, including Pierre Elliott Trudeau and Gérard Pelletier.

CNTU Confederation of National Trade Unions. Before 1961, the Canadian Catholic Confederation of Labour (CCCL). One of Quebec's major trade-union centrals, originally founded as a Catholic alternative to the "dangerous social tendencies" of American-supported unions, but later the main centre of radicalism in the Quebec labour movement. One of the components of the Common Front.

CSD Centrale des Syndicats Démocratiques (Central of Democratic Trade Unions). Quebec trade-union central formed in 1972, after a split in the Confederation of National Trade Unions (CNTU), by the right wing of the CNTU executive.

FLQ At various times Front de Libération du Québec or Front de Libération Québécois. One of a series of organizations, from 1963 to 1971, pursuing an independent Quebec through terrorism. Responsible for the major political bombings and kidnappings.

FRAP Front d'Action Politique. Montreal municipal political party opposing Mayor Jean Drapeau. Composed of a number of Comités d'Action Politique (CAPs).

Hydro-Québec Quebec government hydroelectric power company, vastly expanded after 1962 with the nationalization of the province's private hydro companies. Became a symbol of the Quiet Revolution and Quebec public enterprise in the sixties.

Iron Ore Company of Canada Company formed by a consortium of American steel companies in the 1950s to exploit Quebec iron ore. Opened an iron mine at Schefferville in northern Quebec after generous concessions from Premier Maurice Duplessis.

LIS Ligue pour l'Intégration Scolaire. Before March 1969, Mouvement pour l'Intégration Scolaire (MIS). In the late sixties, a group demanding that French be the only language of instruction in Quebec schools. Originally formed to contest school-board elections in the Montreal suburb of St-Léonard.

MIS See LIS.

MLT Mouvement de Libération du Taxi. Organization formed in 1968 to fight for the interests of Montreal taxi drivers.

Parti Pris Radical nationalist journal of the mid-sixties and a major intellectual influence on the development of the Quebec movement. Still survives as a publishing house.

PQ Parti Québécois. Quebec political party, formed in 1968 by René Lévesque and advocating the political independence of Quebec, obtained through electoral means. Received 24 per cent of the vote in the 1970 election.

Power Corporation of Canada Conglomerate with major media, transport and other holdings in Quebec, and with ties to American and English Canadian capital and both old-line Quebec political parties.

QFL Quebec Federation of Labour. One of Quebec's major trade-union centrals, consisting of the Quebec locals of unions affiliated with the Canadian Labour Congress (CLC), and often with the AFL-CIO in the United States. Before 1971, rival of the Confederation of National Trade

Unions, tending to be more conservative than the CNTU. Later, component of the Common Front with the CNTU and the Quebec Teachers Corporation.

RIN Rassemblement pour l'Indépendance Nationale. Quebec's first large separatist party, formed in 1960. Received nine per cent of the vote in the 1966 election. Dissolved in 1968, with most of its members joining the Parti Québécois (PQ).

St-Jean-Baptiste Society Catholic-nationalist patriotic organization, named after the patron saint of Quebec.

UN Union Nationale. After 1971, Unité-Québec (UQ). Conservative Quebec political party, in power 1936-1939, 1944-1960 and 1966-1970.

UQ See UN.

Appendix 3
Major dates in recent Quebec History

1949 Bitter strike at Asbestos, pitting the labour movement, intellectuals and large parts of the Roman Catholic clergy against the American-owned Johns-Manville Company and the provincial government of Maurice Duplessis; first appearance of the liberal coalition that was to bring down Duplessis.

1952-56 Establishment with substantial help from the provincial government of a huge iron mine at Schefferville in northern Quebec by a consortium of American steel companies and a copper mine at Murdochville in the Gaspé by Toronto-based Noranda Mines Ltd.

1957 Six-month strike at Murdochville that tore Quebec apart as Asbestos had eight years earlier.

1959 *September 18* Death of Duplessis at Schefferville after a fifteen-year reign as premier, opening the way for the defeat of his Union Nationale party.

1960 *June 22* Election of the Liberals under Jean Lesage and beginning of the Quiet Revolution.

October 25 Election of Jean Drapeau as mayor of Montreal with promises to clean up the city.

Formation of the first separatist groups, including the Rassemblement pour l'Indépendance Nationale.

1962 *November 14* Re-election of the Liberals with an increased majority, on a platform of nationalization of Quebec's hydroelectric power companies (pushed by Natural Resources Minister René Lévesque) and a slogan of Maîtres Chez Nòus—Masters in our Own House.

First large nationalist demonstrations of the sixties; protest outside Canadian National Railways headquarters in Montreal against the CNR's lack of a French-Canadian vice-president.

1963 *Spring* Appearance of the first Front de Libération Québécois (FLQ); bombings of federal buildings and mailboxes in English-speaking Westmount; death of one person and maiming of another; capture and imprisonment and beginning of the Lesage government's wide-ranging of FLQ.

1964 Formation of Quebec's first department of education and beginning of the Lesage government's wide-ranging educational reforms.

October 10 "Le samedi de la matraque"—Crushing of the demonstration against Queen Elizabeth's visit to Quebec City.

1965 *May* Resignation of Jean Marchand as president of the Confederation of National Trade Unions (CNTU) and his replacement by Marcel Pepin.

November 8 Election to federal House of Commons as Liberals of the "three wise men"—Jean Marchand, Pierre Elliott Trudeau and Gérard Pelletier—who had been leaders of the anti-Duplessis movement.

1966 *June 5* Defeat of the Lesage Liberals and return of the Union Nationale under Daniel Johnson; nine percent of the vote for RIN.

Second FLQ under ideological leadership of Pierre Vallières and Charles Gagnon; bombings of strikebound plants and two deaths; arrest of Vallières and Gagnon in New York City.

1967 *Spring* Strike by Quebec's Roman Catholic teachers, crushed by the provincial government.

July Visit of President Charles de Gaulle to Quebec and his "Vive le Québec libre!" speech from the balcony of Montreal's City Hall.

October Departure of René Lévesque from the Liberal Party and formation of the Mouvement Souveraineté-Association.

1968 *June* Election of members of the unilinguist Mouvement pour l'Intégration Scolaire to the school board in the Montreal suburb of St-Léonard.

June 24 Large bottle-throwing RIN demonstration in Montreal against St-Jean-Baptiste Day parade appearance of Prime Minister Trudeau, helping to produce Trudeau's large electoral majority the next day.

September 26 Sudden death of Premier Johnson and accession to the premiership of Jean-Jacques Bertrand.

Autumn Reappearance of the FLQ; bombings of Montreal

stock exchange, Noranda Mines office, and other corporate centres.

October Massive revolt of CEGEP students, occupation of school buildings all over the province, and 10,000-strong demonstration in Montreal.

October Unification of MSA and the right-wing Ralliement National to form Parti Québécois; absorption of most of the RIN into the PQ.

October 30 Mouvement de Libération du Taxi (MLT) demonstration at Montreal Airport, with buses overturned and Molotov cocktails thrown.

1969 March 28 Large demonstration in front of the gates of McGill University in Montreal, demanding its conversion into a French-language university.

June 21 Union Nationale congress confirming Bertrand in the premiership; large demonstration outside.

September 10 Demonstration in St-Léonard in support of unilingual schools, ending in the reading of the riot act and charging of three people with sedition.

October 7 One-day strike by Montreal police; MLT demonstration in front of Murray Hill garage; exchange of sniper fire with one person killed; looting and window-breaking in downtown shopping area; calling of federal troops into Montreal.

October 27-31 Huge demonstrations in Montreal and Quebec City against Bill 63, a government measure confirming English as an official language of education.

November 7 Demonstration in Montreal demanding the release of Vallières and Gagnon, including window-breaking in the St. James Street financial district, leading to Drapeau's anti-demonstration bylaw.

1970 Apriil 1 Expiry of contract of Montreal mail-truck drivers—"les gars de Lapalme"—and refusal of federal government to rehire them, setting the stage for long conflict.

April 29 Election of a Liberal government under Robert Bourassa with 72 of the 108 National Assembly seats and 45 per cent of the popular vote after a campaign whose main feature was the surprising strength of the PQ; the PQ was second in the popular vote with 24 per cent but captured only seven seats.

May-June Release of Vallières and Gagnon by new Liberal Justice Minister Jérôme Choquette.

October 5 Kidnapping of British trade commissioner James Cross by the Libération cell of the FLQ and beginning of the October crisis.

October 8 Reading of the FLQ manifesto on Radio-Canada in response to the kidnappers' demand.

October 10 Television statement by Choquette refusing the FLQ's demands; kidnapping of Quebec Labour Minister Pierre Laporte by the Chenier cell of the FLQ.

October 14 Statement by a group of French Canadian moderates calling on the government to meet the FLQ's demands in order to save Cross and Laporte.

October 15 Entry of federal troops into Montreal; mass rally at the Paul Sauvé arena in support of the aims of the FLQ.

October 16 Invocation of the War Measures Act by the federal government; beginning of mass arrests.

October 18 Discovery of Pierre Laporte's body in the trunk of a car.

October 25 Re-election of Jean Drapeau with a clean sweep of Montreal city council seats in a climate of fear and smearing of the main opposition party, FRAP, as a front for the FLQ.

October 26 Launching by the federal government and the Toronto *Star* of the rumour that a group of moderate Quebecers planned to establish a provisional government.

December 1 Replacement of the War Measures Act by the Public Order (Temporary Measures) Act.

December 3 Acceptance of a deal by the Libération cell allowing Cross to be freed and the kidnappers to be flown to Cuba.

December 28 Capture of the Chenier cell.

1971 *Winter-spring* Series of trials on political charges of people arrested under the War Measures Act; almost all were acquitted.

April 30 Expiry of Public Order Act and restoration of civil liberties to Quebec for the first time in six months.

July Beginning of a lockout at the Montreal newspaper *La Presse* in a conflict that was eventually to involve the whole Quebec labour movement.

October 29 Mass demonstration of solidarity with *La Presse* employees headed by the three leaders of the Quebec labour movement—Louis Laberge, Marcel Pepin and Yvon

Charbonneau—broken up by police beatings and clubbings; death of one demonstrator.

November 2 Mass rally at the Montreal Forum establishing the Common Front of labour and vowing to fight the regime.

November Quebec Federation of Labour convention and release of working papers entitled *L'état, rouage de notre exploitation* (The state is our exploiter); militant speech by Laberge.

Autumn Release of the CNTU manifesto. *Ne Comptons que sur nos propres moyens*, calling for the overthrow of capitalism.

December Decision by chief FLQ ideologue Pierre Vallières to renounce terrorism and support the Parti Québécois.

1972 March 28 One-day general strike by 210,000 civil servants united in a Common Front over deadlocked contract negotiations with the provincial government.

April 11 Beginning of all-out civil-service strike; injunctions by the government against hospital workers.

April 19 Thirteen hospital workers sentenced to fines and jail terms for defying injunctions.

April 21 Passage of Bill 19 legislating the civil servants back to work; decision by the Common Front to accept Bill 19 and end the strike.

May 8 Sentencing of Laberge, Pepin and Charbonneau to a year in jail each for defying injunctions.

May 9 Demonstration in Quebec City as Laberge, Pepin and Charbonneau turned themselves in.

May 9-18 Strikes and demonstrations in Sept-Iles, St-Jérôme and other towns and cities across the province protesting the jailing of the union leaders and Bill 19.

May 23 Decision by Laberge, Pepin, Charbonneau and other imprisoned unionists to appeal their sentences and accept release on bail.

May Split in CNTU between supporters of Pepin and those of the conservative "three Ds".

Also from James Lewis & Samuel . . .

Up against City Hall

Toronto's most controversial alderman, John Sewell, provides a behind-the-scenes account of how city politics really works. Paper $2.95

Canada's Water: For Sale?

Journalist Dick Bocking lays bare the water development plans of Canadian agencies and governments, and explains how they threaten to lead to massive exports of water to the U.S. Cloth $6.95

She Named It Canada

A witty, entertaining, attractive illustrated history of Canada written by the Corrective Collective, a Vancouver-based women's group. Paper 50¢

A History of Canadian Wealth

Gustavus Myers' classic of Canadian economic and political history-writing, exposing our own home-grown robber barons and con-men, the wheelers and dealers in land and votes and lives. Written in 1913 and never before published in Canada, Myers' book has been acclaimed. Paper $2.95

Quebec in Question

A short, lucid separatist's history of Quebec written by sociologist Marcel Rioux and translated by James Boake. Paper $3.50

The Citizens' Guide to City Politics

The first practical and realistic guide to how city hall operates and why, which focusses on the links between city government and the real estate and land development industry. Written by James Lorimer. Paper $3.95